Dedicated to the loved ones of the author

For Carolin, Anike and Ferdinand

Karl Michael Popp

Mergers and Acquisitions
in the
Software Industry

Foundations of due diligence

Impressum

Bibliografische Information der Deutschen Nationalbibliothek

Die Deutsche Nationalbibliothek verzeichnet diese Publikation in der Deutschen Natio-nalbibliografie; detaillierte bibliografische Daten sind im Internet über http://dnb.d-nb.de abrufbar.

Herstellung und Verlag: BoD - Books on Demand, Norderstedt

ISBN-13: 9783848221998

Cover by www.plan33.de

Disclaimer

Copyright © 2013 Dr. Karl Popp

Table of Contents

Quote

"The most active and successful technology M&A acquirers pursue extensive due diligence to assess the potential risks of a particular acquisition.

This includes a detailed review of a potential target's products and underlying technology, customer/partner opportunities, contracts & obligations, assessment of the target's employees, and a detailed review of a company's business model & financial position, among other areas.

Many acquirers will have very large teams and a highly structured way to go about this process, which (along with the large volumes of information that is typically requested) creates a very demanding and time consuming process for a potential seller.

So potential targets need to prepare for this process well in advance of receiving an LOI by gathering the key due diligence information and populating a data room that an acquirer can look at on "Day 1" of the diligence process.

Advance preparation can streamline the due diligence process and sends a strong signal to the acquirer that the target is serious about getting a transaction done."

Scott Card

Scott Card is a partner in the Investment Banking group at AGC Partners, focused on enterprise infrastructure, including storage, cloud/virtualization, big data, and security. In his 18+ years as an investment banker, Scott has completed more than 50 mergers and acquisitions (M&A) and equity/debt financing transactions. Prior to joining AGC Partners, Scott was part of Deutsche Bank Alex. Brown's Technology Investment Banking Group in Boston, Associate in Mergers & Acquisitions at SBC Warburg and an Analyst in the Financial Institutions Group at Merrill Lynch & Co.

1. Introduction

1.1 Why this book

Goal of this book is to provide you with key knowledge and skills for successful due diligence in the software industry. You will learn about the M&A process, M&A organization, due diligence coverage, due diligence hacks and specifics of the software industry, like business models, software ecosystems and partnership models.

For me to write this book, there are three reasons: Recent business modeling knowledge is not represented in M&A books, increasing presence of software in consumer goods creates the demand for software M&A knowledge in all industries and merger integration is not covered well as a strategic goal of and in activities in due diligence.

Business modeling knowledge desperately needed

In M&A literature i did not find recent information systems research and business modeling represented there. In addition, the specifics of the software industry like software business models and software ecosystems, are not covered sufficiently.

Software is everywhere

With the increasing proliferation of software in all kinds of goods it is paramount to gain insights into the specifics of the software industry and how we do proper due diligence of software companies and software products. This is what this book is dedicated to.

Merger integration as a goal in due diligence

Successful acquirers start early with planning the integration and look in detail at merger integration risk. Starting early means that during due diligence, integration planning and integration risk management activities

Introduction

are executed. This book shows how the integration related activities are done in due diligence to ensure integration success.

Discuss and share your feedback at http://www.mergerduediligence.com.

Follow me on twitter @karl_popp. https://twitter.com/karl_popp

Connect with me on linkedin: de.linkedin.com/in/drkarlmichaelpopp/

1.2   Goals of this book

This book series has four simple goals:

> Goal #1: This book tries to create a holistic view of mergers and acquisitions in the software industry and to introduce post merger integration planning as an integral part of due diligence of software companies.

A holistic view allows to find analogies and differences between companies in the software industry, but also between companies in the software industry and other companies.

A holistic view needs a holistic model, where popular views like finance, controlling, commercial views are just projections of the holistic model.

We will use a business modeling approach to reach the goal. We will present typical partnership models and delivery models, which will allow us to identify analogies between different companies, partnerships and delivery models.

> Goal # 2: This book tries to point out the key differentiators of the software industry to other industries, like

- ❏ Products and services,
- ❏ Business models,
- ❏ Ecosystem strategies,
- ❏ Intellectual property management and
- ❏ Frequency and speed of disruption and technological innovation.

Introduction

> Goal # 3: This book tries to lay the foundation for standardization of due diligence activities for software companies and to build a foundation for successful post merger integration planning in the due diligence phase.

If we reach these goals in this book and in our profession, we get closer to sustainable post merger integration results and to a higher likelihood of success of M&A activities.

> Goal #4: This book focuses on aspeccts of business models and software industry specifics for due diligence.

In this book we will get very deep into new and software specific aspects like business models, ecosystems and intellectual property due diligence. As a consequence, we will leave details on financial, tax, IT and HR due diligence to other books and authors.

1.3 A big thank you

I would like to thank you for buying this book. Many people have helped in gathering the knowledge that is the foundation of this book. First and foremost, I would like to thank my colleagues in the SAP corporate development team. I love to work with them on M&A projects as well as improvements of the M&A process. The work with them is fun and a continuing inspiration to make things better. In addition I would like to thank my colleagues from the Global Licensing department at SAP AG for working with me on open source and third party related due diligence activities.

Another big thank you goes to my colleagues that work together with me on a curriculum for a master study on post merger integration. They come from german companies Beiersdorf, EON, Deutsche Bahn, Siemens, Dekra, Bosch, to name a few. The meetings and discussions with them allowed me to testdrive a lot of my ideas. Also, many thanks go to Dr. Josef Waltl for giving me advice on providing short summaries for each chapter.

Introduction

In addition, cudos go to Ralf Meyer of Synomic, one of the finest consulting companies for software companies. He is a great supporter of my work and has offered to make this book part of the Synomic academy.

Last but not least I would like to thank my wonderful family and my friends for supporting me in this effort.

1.4 Chapters of this book

Let us quickly run through the contents of this book.

Economic foundations

This section introduces research results from information systems research about modeling of companies as business systems and its application to mergers and acquisitions. Since this knowledge has not been used on M&A, I am trying to make you aware of this recent development.

Foundations of mergers and acquisitions

This chapter introduces key terminology and characteristics of mergers and acquisitions and explains how companies setup up organization and processes to execute mergers and acquisitions. I will take a constructive approach and provide concise definitions to make sure you understand the details.

Foundations of due diligence

Due diligence is a task within the M&A process. In this chapter the task is defined and different types of due diligences are presented. Then, due diligence is analysed being a modeling activity. This allows to find some blind spots and typical sources of trouble in due diligence and post merger integration and gets you prepared for running due diligence.

Introduction

Handling risks in merger due diligence

Since M&A projects have a bad reputation due to many failures, risk detection and management is an important task. In this section, we learn a new approach for detection of risk and get to know how risks are handled afterwards.

Foundations of the software business

This section gives you important insights into the intrinsics of the software business. It shows which business models and revenue models are part of a software vendor´s business and which other patterns of business like delivery models exist in the software business. We will use these patterns to attach typical success factors, risks, goals to these patterns for due diligence. We will also drill into IP Due diligence and specific risks in software business models.

Foundations of software ecosystems

One special aspect of software vendors is their ecosystems of suppliers and partners and customers. This section shows which types of software ecosystems exist and how they are leveraged by software vendors to create revenue and extend their solution offering.

Partnership models in the software industry

From resell to revenue share and online solution marketplaces there are many different types of partner relationships. Each of these relationships can make sense for a software vendor.

1.5 Hacking due diligence: a fun introduction

Please take the content of this section seriously. It sounds funny, but it is derived from the experience of many due diligences.

Introduction

Due Diligence Rule 1: Everybody lies.

No kidding, enough tell tales in this world. Getting as much hard facts as possible, is the most important rule. If somebody tells you to cross the road with closed eyes, fine. You better check the facts.

This rule courtesy of Dr. Gregory House. This time, watching TV made a lot of sense.

Due diligence Rule 2: break them before they break you

Set M&A deal breakers to sleep. identify from catalogue of 50 deal breakers. attack, put to sleep, done.

Due Diligence Rule 3: Maximize the likelihood of success.

Do you recall statistics? you don´t know the distribution, so 50 percent chance of success is the maximum likelihood best guess. work your way up! get the key success factors during due diligence and monitor them frequently.

Due Diligence Rule 4: Minimize deal risk and find sleep

Identify from a catalogue of 200 risks during due diligence. Identify, mitigate, monitor, done. For some risk: sell them to insurance companies and have somebody else loose their sleep.

Due diligence rule 5: Make your day. Blueprint.

What will life be like on day one? What are the steps/changes/challenges in the first 100 days? What are the goals 12/18/24 months from now? When will integration be done? You better know it. Blueprint it at the end of due diligence!

Due diligence rule 6: Look in the mirror (not the rear view mirror, stupid!)

Look at yourself (the acquiring company) in due diligence. What happens to the acquiring company due to the impact of the acquired company? Will the workload of the post merger integration hit too hard? What will the efforts be? You better use the results of due diligence to determine the impact and plan additional resources.

Due diligence rule 7: Safeguard your property

So you are acquiring intellectual property. Great. But do you really own it? Can you really monetize it later? Run IP Due diligence to check all intellectual property of the target. If needed, establish additional IP rights. Then start monetizing post close.

Due diligence rule 8: You have all the facts. NOT.

The facts are transported. Somebody tells you facts, but forgot something. You hear the facts, but you are not sure you understood. Guess what is left from the original facts. NOTHING.

2. Economic foundations: Business Models

Financial modeling of businesses is around for a long time. Semantic business modeling is not. Since none of the semantic, graphical business modeling approaches has made its way into due diligence, this chapter tries to provide basics on this method for modeling businesses.

Having read this chapter you will own background knowledge about modeling businesses and about fundamental properties of businesses as systems. This knowledge will help you in due diligence to better cope with different businesses you analyze.

2.1 Analyzing companies as a model building process

Model building is a process of looking at the real world and creating a simplified view of the world. In this simplified view, we include assumptions about the real world and we omit some of the complexity of the real world. Many different abstraction mechanism can be applied to the real world when building the model. One important one is type building. Another one is omission. So if we look at a company to be acquired, we might just look at the employees to serve the purpose of human resources due diligence.

Looking at software companies and building models of software companies, we will look at specifics that make software companies different from companies in other industries. First and foremost, software companies are companies that strive for commercial success by offering their products and services to the customers in their target markets. For doing that, they rely on suppliers to provide products and services to them.

Model building

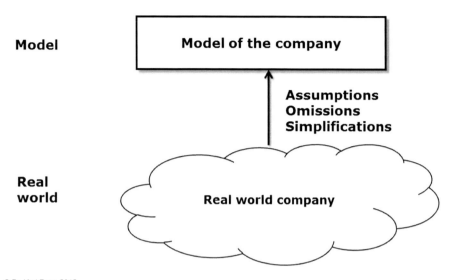

Figure 1: Model building

There are payments made to compensate for the products and services provided and received. From this viewpoint, there is no difference between a software company and companies in other industries, which allows us to leverage due diligence approaches from other industries to a certain degree. This viewpoint also allows us to identify the main differences to other industries and to define specific due diligence methods, processes and tools to address these differences.

Example

Figure 2 contains a simple model of a software vendor interacting with its environment. In this figure we omit other interactions of the software vendor with its environment, like with tax authorities, shareholders, patent holders etc. We also simplify the real world by looking at all suppliers and customers collectively in the model elements Suppliers and Customers.

Interaction model of the Business Strategy and business plan layer

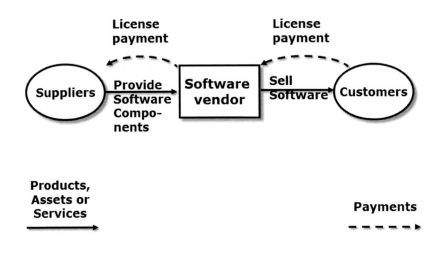

Figure 2: Simple model of a software vendor

2.2 Modeling companies as business systems

In this section we use an approach to look at companies as business systems. We are particularly interested in the structural and behavioral properties of business systems. The method presented here is based on [1] and extends and comments this approach.

Companies as business systems

The Semantic Object Model (SOM) is an approach for modeling of business systems and views a business system from a system theory viewpoint as an open, goal-driven, socio-technical system [1].

Openness of business systems

A business system is an **open system**, not closed, since it interacts with its environment by exchanging products, services and payments. Figure 3 shows the interactions of a software vendor with its environment.

Interactions of a software vendor as a business system

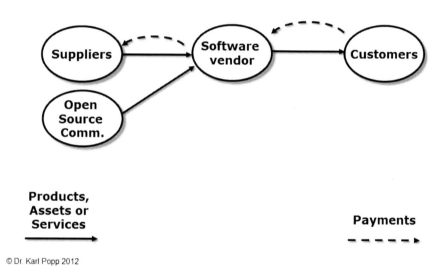

© Dr. Karl Popp 2012

Figure 3: Interaction of a business system with its environment

So what is the impact of openness? For a business system this means that business activities of entities outside of the business system have impact on the business system. Planning activities, like orders to suppliers, inventory management and other activities have to be coordinated between the business system and the outside entities. This makes planning tasks more complex and creates dependencies to entities outside of the business. ness.

Economic foundations: Business Models

Example

In Figure 3 the impact of openness can be as follows

☐ *The relationship to the open source community creates an opportunity in being able to use open source software, but it also creates a dependency, since the software vendor is relying on the open source community to deliver quality products on time.*

☐ *Using open source software creates a dependency to the license terms of the open source software used.*

☐ *The relationship with the customer creates dependencies, since the incoming customer orders have impact on fulfillment planning.*

☐ *The relationship with suppliers creates an impact on planning of software development activities since the software vendor assumes that the supplier will provide quality software on time and quality and coordination has to happen to create a joint schedule of software development activities.*

As recent research shows, openness can be advantageous, like in open innovation, where the openness of one company attracts other companies for increased business of both companies.

Business Systems are goal-driven

A business system is a **goal-driven system**, since goals exist that the business system tries to achieve. The achievement of goals is done via execution of business processes inside of the business system. Business processes, no matter if they are automated or not, view the behavior of the business system. We differentiate between Goals, which specify the goods and services provided by the business system, and Objectives, which measure business performance. Figure 4 shows an example for goals and objectives of a software vendor.

Since business systems are goal-driven, it makes perfect sense to include goals in due diligence. Goals also drive the execution in business systems.

So if you are planning to realize synergies, the synergies must have supporting goals to become reality.

A goal-driven business system

Figure 4: A goal-driven business system

Business systems are socio-technical systems

A business system is also a **socio-technical system** since the interaction between customers, partners and the resources of the business system like employees and technical items like machines, plants and application software is used to achieve the goals of the business system. This implies interfaces between companies, users and application systems as well as coordination between users and application systems.

Dynamics of business systems

Business systems and their environments are constantly changing. It is important to keep that in mind when talking about due diligence. The result of the due diligence shows the status of the analyzed company at a given point in time. Assumptions were taken for that given point in time. Changes over time may take place in the target company but also in the acquiring company. Customers, suppliers, partners and competitors as well as regulatory authorities might change over time, too. So the assumptions taken at a certain point in time may not be valid in the future due to business dynamics.

Here are some examples for dynamics that impact business systems:

Type of dynamics	Impact
Strategy dynamics	Strategy has high volatility over time, in the software industry we see also dynamics and high impact of platform strategies and partner ecosystems.
Market dynamics	Products, customers and partners may change. In the software industry, we have additional dynamics due to high frequency and speed of product disruptions in markets.
Business model dynamics	In the software industry, we see high change rate and diversity of business models, revenue models and their combinations.
Technological dynamics	High change rate of software platforms and other technology may cause disruptions.
Resource dynamics	Presence of employees for only short time periods (about 2 years) in the software industry is challenging. Rapid technological change also often drives organizational change.

Economic foundations: Business Models

External factors	Business related laws and regulations may change.

There is no general solution how to deal with dynamics, but you can keep track of dynamics and time-dependent assumptions in a model based approach to due diligence. The model is your store and retrieval mechanism to cope with dynamics.

Example

When your task is to do due diligence on a target company and later to acquire and integrate the target into the acquiring company, Figure 5 shows the time dynamics. While the due diligence of a target company takes place at time t=1, the post merger integration starts at t=2. The question arises, what internal and external changes have taken place that might impact the success of the post merger integration. In addition, the acquiring company might have changed structure and behavior, like changed organization, changed strategy etc.

Business System dynamics and due diligence

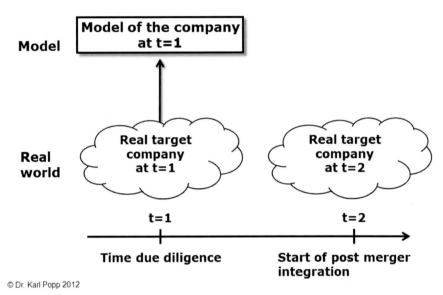

© Dr. Karl Popp 2012

Figure 5: Business system dynamics and due diligence

Dynamics impact planning. Human beings have trouble anticipating the impact of dynamics, especially if the dynamics are non-linear. So it makes sense to look in detail into dynamics and their impact to better cope with dynamics of business systems.

Complexity of business systems

Lucks presents a complexity model used at Siemens that shows a number of proposed dimensions that make up a model of complexity of post merger integration projects. We can use it in part to determine the complexity of a business system. Regarding the underlying business systems, there are two categories of dimensions of business systems, **Volume** and **Structural Complexity** (Figure 6).

Economic foundations: Business Models

Complexity of business systems

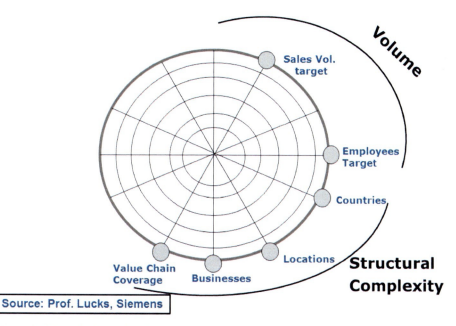

Figure 6: Complexity of business systems

Structural complexity has the dimensions

☐ Number of countries the target operates in;

☐ Number of locations the target operates in;

☐ Number of businesses the target operates;

☐ Coverage of the value chain in the industry the target operates in;

Volume has the dimensions

☐ Sales volume of acquiring business unit;

☐ Sales volume of target business unit;

☐ Number of employees of acquiring business unit;

Economic foundations: Business Models

❒ Number of employees of target business unit.

Before we look at completeness of this complexity model, let us have a look at two examples: the acquisitions of a large and a medium sized software vendor.

Complexity of business systems: Examples

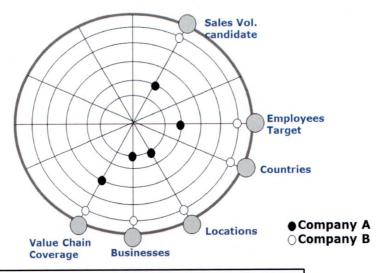

Source: Chart: Prof. Lucks, Siemens, Examples: Dr. Karl Popp

Figure 7: Example for business system complexity

Example

All information for this example was taken from real acquisition cases and anonymized. Company A was a medium size software vendor, while Company B is a large software vendor.

In a corresponding chart for these two acquisitions, we clearly see different values in each of the dimensions. The idea is to get a notion of the complexity of the business systems by taking the area covered by

Economic foundations: Business Models

the graph that connects all the data points. In Figure 7 you see that the area covered by the Company B graph is bigger than the Company A graph leading to the assumption that the complexity and effort of the Company B business system might be bigger than the complexity of the Company A business system.

Critical view at the complexity model

This model is a good start to look at complexity. Intuitively, there are the following weaknesses of this complexity model.

❏ Only structural complexity is taken into account, except the value chain coverage, which shows how much of the value chain in the industry is covered by the target;

❏ Only sales volume and employee numbers make up the volume measures. The question is, if there are additional measures of volume, like the number of produced items or the number of deals that lead to the sales volume.

I will propose a hopefully better complexity model later in this book.

2.3   Enterprise architecture and models of business systems

Let us use an approach for modeling of business systems. What we would like to achieve with this is:

❏ Completeness of business models by providing a modeling approach that is close to reality and allows checks for completeness;

❏ Formalized modeling of the structure and relationships of the businesses;

❏ Semantic annotations of the business model with items like issues, risks, critical success factors, synergies etc.

❏ Continuous learning and reuse of business models for due diligence: If there are generic models or analogies between models created in

Economic foundations: Business Models

due diligences of different companies, we would like to learn from and reuse models and semantic annotations from these due diligence projects.

Business systems are complex. Complexity calls for abstraction mechanisms. The approach to be presented uses different abstraction mechanisms. The most important one is the Enterprise Architecture (Ferstl, 1997) which has three layers. Figure 8, taken and adapted from Ferstl and Sinz, shows the different layers. The first layer provides an outside view of the business system, defines goals of the business system and its interactions with the environment.

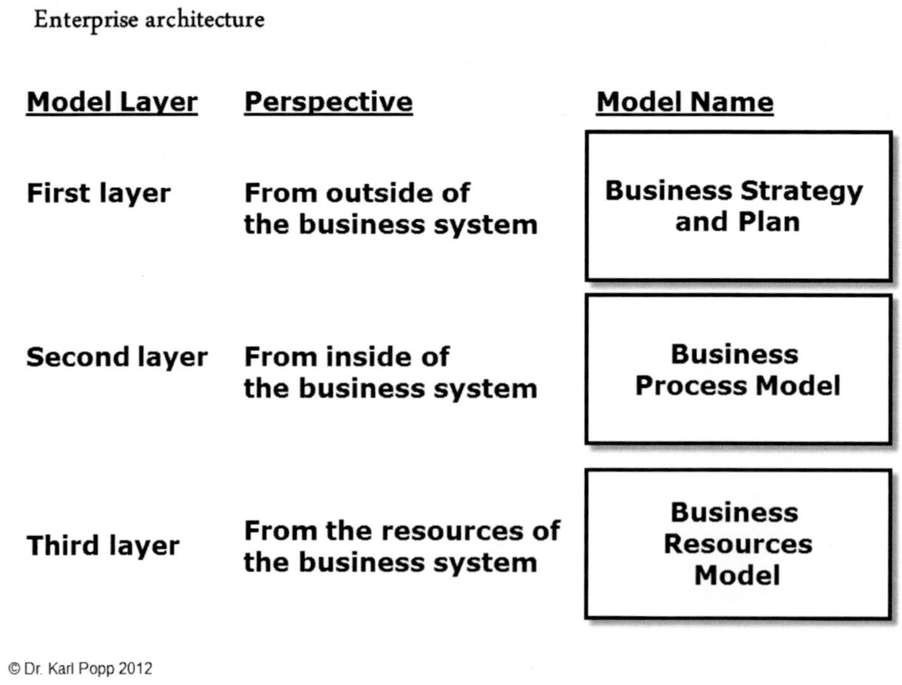

Enterprise architecture

Model Layer	Perspective	Model Name
First layer	From outside of the business system	Business Strategy and Plan
Second layer	From inside of the business system	Business Process Model
Third layer	From the resources of the business system	Business Resources Model

© Dr. Karl Popp 2012

Figure 8: Enterprise architecture (1)

The second layer takes an inside view at the business system and analyses the structure and behavior inside the business system. The behavior defines the business processes and their execution. Figure 8 shows layers, perspectives and model names.

The third layer looks at resources of the business system, like organizations, employees or machines, but it also looks at application systems. It is important to notice, that until you reach the third layer, you do not look at resources of the business system.

So why do we leverage this approach? The approach presented here gives us several levels of abstraction, which allow for a reduction of complexity and separation of concerns in analyzing companies as business systems. As you can see in the three layers, the first one is an abstraction from everything that is inside the business system (including the business resources). The second layer abstracts from the business resources. The third layer abstracts the business resources from the business processes. Links between the layers allow for a holistic model. Using these links, you can assign goals from the strategy to business processes and resources from the third layer to business processes of the second layer. Later on, we will see that certain tasks of the due diligence also relate only to certain layers of the Enterprise Architecture.

Business Strategy and business plan layer

The business strategy and business plan layer contains the outside view of the company under consideration. It contains a structural view on a type level that shows the modeled company and its interaction with the customers, partners, suppliers and authorities.

Economic foundations: Business Models

Interaction model of the Business Strategy and business plan layer

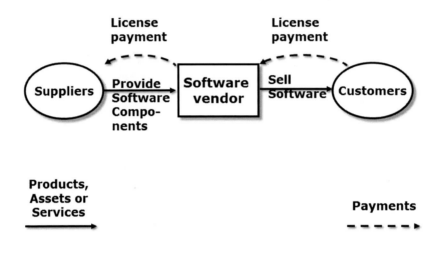

© Dr. Karl Popp 2012

Figure 9: Interaction model

Example

For an example, please see Figure 9. The company under considera-tion is a software vendor. We can see the software vendor and its rela-tionships to the outside world in the form of type level product, asset or services relationships as well as payment relationships. The soft-ware vendor sells software to its customers and gets license fees in re-turn. The software vendors uses components from its suppliers to cre-ate the software sold to its customers and pays a license fee to the suppliers for using the solutions.

And the first layer also contains a dynamic view that defines the behavior of the company in the form of the business strategy and overall task of the company.

Economic foundations: Business Models

A goal-driven business system

Figure 10: Overall task of a software vendor

Example

A software vendor has an overall task as described in Figure 10. The overall purpose of the company is to create and sell software while trying to maximize profit.

Based on our modeling approach a business strategy is a set of goals that describe future states of objects and relationships of the interaction diagram. A business strategy is complete if there is one or more goals for each of the objects and the relationships of the interaction model.

Economic foundations: Business Models

Example

The strategy of the software vendor is derived from the interaction model in Figure 9. The software vendor needs strategies for each object and each relationship in the interaction model. Product strategy relates to the relationship to the customer, market strategy relates to the customer object, supplier strategy relates to the supplier object, corporate strategy to the object software vendor etc.

Figure 11 shows a more complex example of a business strategy. The business strategy here is not complete, since not all objects and relationships have goals defined.

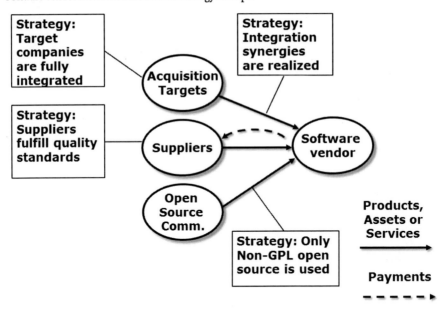

Software vendor interaction model and strategy example

© Dr. Karl Popp 2013

Figure 11: Business strategy example

Business process model layer

For due diligence, the business process model allows to analyze the business on a high level, while also allowing to drill down into more detail. The acquirer can already view and select the parts of the business he would like to continue, change or discontinue.

The business process model layer takes an inside view at the business system and analyses the structure and behavior inside the business system.

Two views are applied: a structure view showing the tasks and their decomposition and a behavior view showing the execution of the tasks as part of business processes.

Structure view

The structure view is identical with the interaction model that we already have used in this book. In addition to the high level interaction models we have seen, the structure view also allows decomposition of objects and interactions between these objects.

Example

In the interaction model in Figure 12 we see the object software vendor interacting with the objects Suppliers and Customers. To homogenize the processing of the interactions, we could decompose the software vendor object into a development team object handling the supplier relationship and providing the products to be sold and a sales object handling the interaction with the object Customer.

Economic foundations: Business Models

Interaction model of the Business Strategy and business plan layer

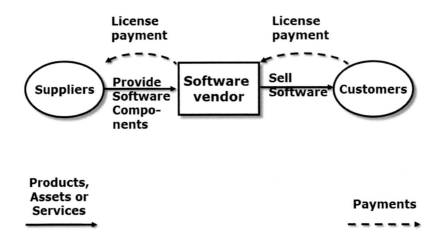

© Dr. Karl Popp 2012

Figure 12: Interaction model

Behavior model

The behavior model shows the tasks that allow the coordination of goods, assets, services exchanged between objects in the interaction model. So if software components are provided by a supplier to a software vendor, there are at least two tasks to be modeled, one for providing the software component and one for receiving the software component.

Example

Figure 13 shows the behavior model that corresponds to Figure 9. The supplier ships the software to the software vendor, the software vendor receives the software. After that the software vendor pays license fees and the supplier receives the license fees.

Economic foundations: Business Models

Business process model (behavior view)

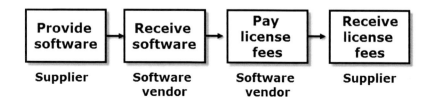

© Dr. Karl Popp 2012

Figure 13: Business process model: behavior view

The behavior model also contains the task decomposition that follows business processes. Figure 14 shows the decomposition of tasks in our example.

Business process model (Task decomposition)

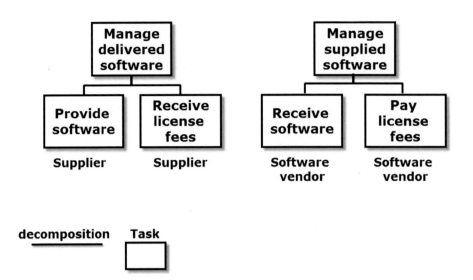

© Dr. Karl Popp 2012

Figure 14: Business process model: task decomposition

Describing tasks in the behaviour model

Tasks can be described in more detail than shown above. The following attributes are available: task object model, goals, objectives, preconditions, postconditions. The task object model contains all objects, services, goods, products that are related to a specific task.

Example

The task Provide software is located at the supplier and send the flow of products called "Provide software" to the software vendor. So the task object model contains the objects Supplier, Software vendor and the flow Provide software.

Task object model of the task Provide software

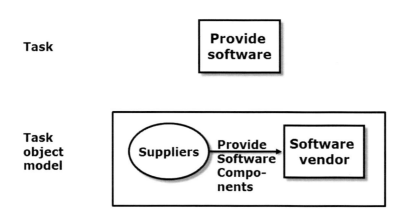

Figure 15: Business process model: task decomposition

Goals describe the end state of the task, defined as a combination of states of the objects in the task object model.

Objectives measure business performance, meaning how well the goals of a tasks are achieved.

Business resources layer

Business resources are all items that are needed to execute the business process model, like the employees, the suppliers, customers and partners of the company under consideration; but also the locations the target operates in and the businesses the target operates as well as all IT equipment that is used.

All these resources are modeled in the business resources layer in the following sections:

❏ People (who are assigned to a certain business and locations and a place within the corporate organizational structure),

❏ Businesses (incorporated entities),

❏ Locations (including facilities, offices, plants and its machinery),

❏ Countries (the target operates in or has locations in) and

❏ Intellectual property.

Example

From the resources model, you can build several views that are familiar, like an HR view showing all the employees and their managers, an IT view that shows all IT equipment and a shop floor view that shows all machine equipment in a production plant. Also possible is a location based view showing all equipment, buildings, people and IT equipment of a location.

A complexity model for business systems based on the enterprise architecture

Based on our enterprise architecture, we are able to model structural and behavioral complexity and we can differentiate and model complexity on different levels of abstraction. Based on the layers of the Enterprise Architecture, we can talk about the complexity of the business strategy and business plan, the complexity of the business process model and the complexity of the business resources.

Complexity and Enterprise architecture

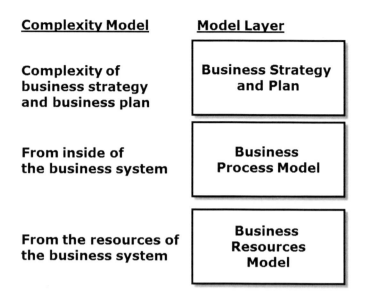

© Dr. Karl Popp 2012

Figure 16: Complexity and Enterprise Architecture

But what is the complexity in each of these layers? Let us look into more detail into each of the layers. On each layer we have a structural and a behavioral view, which are integrated via a common metamodel. We can look at complexity of these two views on each level, which creates the six complexity models which are listed in Figure 17.

Economic foundations: Business Models

Complexity on Enterprise architecture layers

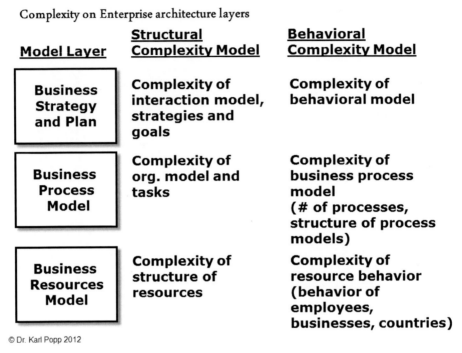

Model Layer	Structural Complexity Model	Behavioral Complexity Model
Business Strategy and Plan	Complexity of interaction model, strategies and goals	Complexity of behavioral model
Business Process Model	Complexity of org. model and tasks	Complexity of business process model (# of processes, structure of process models)
Business Resources Model	Complexity of structure of resources	Complexity of resource behavior (behavior of employees, businesses, countries)

© Dr. Karl Popp 2012

Figure 17: Complexity on each layer of the Enterprise Architecture

2.4 Takeaways from chapter 2

Using models for businesses allows us to create a more complete view of the businesses. By differentiating different model layers, like business strategy layer, business process model and business resources model, we can reduce complexity in the analysis and focus better on specific issues within the layers.

We introduced interaction models in this chapter. In this book, we will make massive use of interaction model diagrams to ensure we have a complete and consistent view of the company under consideration. We also introduced a complexity model. Complexity is a key challenge in due diligence and in planning an executing post merger integration. This

Economic foundations: Business Models

is why knowledge about complexity and about how to handle complexity is key for due diligence.

Economic foundations: Business Models

3. Foundations of mergers and acquisitions

With the knowledge about modeling companies we now look at the specifics of one company acquiring or merging with another company. Now two companies are in the game and this fact is a source of additional considerations.

Having read this chapter, you will know all the terms you need to discuss M&A, the process and the potential pitfalls of executing mergers and acquisitions.

3.1 Definition of mergers and acquisitions based on the Enterprise Architecture

Design of the new entity as a modeling activity

In the light of merger integration, a new entity is created either by integrating the target into the acquiring organization or by creating a new organization from the target and the acquiring company. We leverage the enterprise architecture to show what exactly this means.

Definition of acquisition

Acquisition means that the acquiring company gets ownership of the target company as a whole or of a defined set of assets formerly owned by the target company. Acquisition itself does not state if and how the target will be integrated into the acquiring company.

According to the enterprise architecture, getting ownership means that you get ownership of the business resources and you get information about the business process model and the business strategy and the business plan.

Definition of acquisition

Acquiring company

> Business Strategy and Plan

> Business Process Model

> Business Resources

↓ **has ownership**

Target

> Business Strategy and Plan

> Business Process Model

> Business Resources

© Dr. Karl Popp 2012

Figure 18: Acquisition definition

Definition of merger and merger integration

Merger means that an acquisition has taken place and a merged organization shall be built from an acquiring company and a target company. The process of actually building the merged organization is called merger integration.

Definition of merger

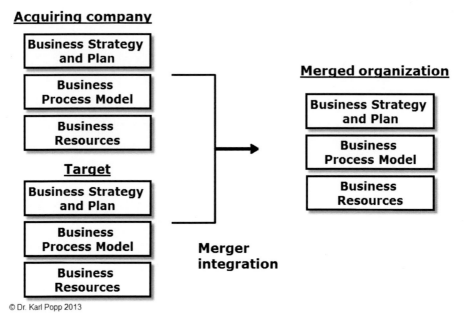

© Dr. Karl Popp 2013

Figure 19: Merger definition

According to the enterprise architecture the following activities have to occur in due diligence and merger integration planning:

☐ Design the new entity: a business strategy and a business plan for the new company is created and the existing business strategy and plan of the target and the acquiring company are converted to the new business strategy. The existing business processes from target and acquiring company are converted to the new business processes. Business resources models from the target and the acquiring company are combined to create the business resources model for the new company.

☐ Plan merger integration: a strategy and a business plan for merger integration as well as a business process model for merger integration

Page 50

is created (or reused from other merger integrations) and a resource model for the merger integration is created.

❏ Execute merger integration: Resources for merger integration are allocated and the merger integration is executed according to the business process model.

Decomposing the merger integration task

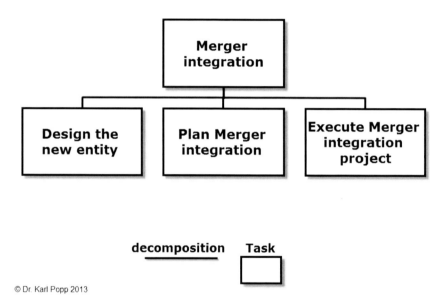

© Dr. Karl Popp 2013

Figure 20: Tasks of merger integration

These are the three main tasks of merger integration. You have to carry out all three to have a complete merger integration. Neglecting one of the three tasks has significant risks.

3.1   Transaction details and deal types

Questions to be answered in this section are: How does an acquiring company take ownership of target companies and their assets? What are the parts of an M&A transaction if you decompose it?

Transaction details

If we look into an acquisition transaction, we really have two transactions taking place: the purchasing transaction and the compensation for that purchasing, usually a payment. In the purchasing transaction, there are usually two types of goods acquired: shares or assets, which will be discussed below. By combining different forms of goods acquired and compensation, you can create many different forms of acquisition transactions.

Regarding compensation, there are many different options like

❏ Share compensation,

❏ Cash compensation and

❏ Earn out compensation.

Acquisition transactions

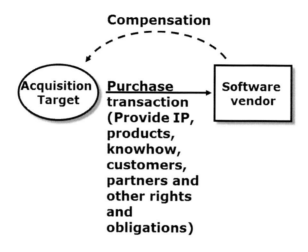

© Dr. Karl Popp 2012

Figure 21: Acquisition transaction details

Asset deal

An asset deal is the acquisition of assets. Assets are specific material and immaterial goods, which are owned by a company.

Share deal

Shares are ownership rights in a company. A share deal is the acquisition of shares. In a share deal, these ownership rights are acquired by the acquiring company.

Pros and cons of asset and share deals

It is important to know the differences and the advantages and disadvantages of the different deal types. The following table is a translated citation to the book from Beiners (Beiners 2009).

Topics	Asset Deal	Share Deal
Assets	Selected assets are acquired.	All assets are acquired.
Liabilities	Selected liabilities are acquired. Exceptions might apply when full businesses are acquired.	All liabilities, even the ones that are not disclosed
Complexity of purchase transaction	High	low
Cash flow	Serves the acquirer	Still serves the target company
Transfer of liabilities	With consent of creditor	Without consent of creditor.
Contracts transfer	Only with consent of contracting parties. Exception might be employment contracts.	Without consent of contracting parties. Exception are change of control clauses in contracts.

Here, we spare further details on tax handling and financing differences between asset deal and share deal.

Merger types

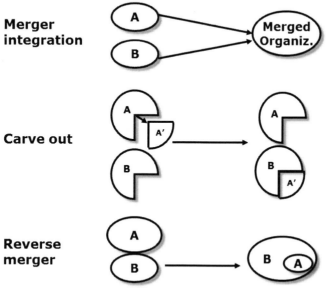

© Dr. Karl Popp 2013

Figure 22: Merger types

Carve out

A part of one entity gets extracted from it and is often later implanted into another entity (see Figure 22). Just like an organ transplant, this is a tricky operation with high risk. You have to make sure you see all the extract's links when extracting and connecting these links into the new organization.

Reverse merger

One entity A acquires entity B. A gets integrated into B then. In this case, usually a smaller entity integrates a larger entity.

Foundations of mergers and acquisitions

Merger integration

Two entities are combined to build a merged organization. One entity has ownership of the other entity.

3.2 Merger integration

Let us look in more detail at merger integration by looking at the overall task and its decomposition.

Merger integration task

The goal of the merger integration task is to build a merged organization by integrating the target organization into a new or existing entity.

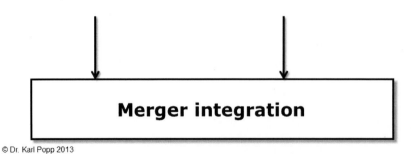

Merger integration task

Goal

Integrate acquired entity into new entity

Objectives

Minimize risk
Continue business
Maximize likelihood of integration success

Merger integration

© Dr. Karl Popp 2013

Figure 23: Merger integration task

Foundations of mergers and acquisitions

Popular objectives are to minimize risk, continue business and to maximize likelihood of integration success or maximizing of synergies.

Decomposition of the task

In most mergers, the merger integration tasks is decomposed into three subtasks:

☐ Design the new entity,

☐ Plan merger integration,

☐ Execute merger integration project.

Decomposing the merger integration task

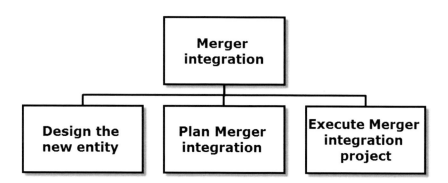

Figure 24: Decomposition of the merger integration task

Frequent acquirers tend to run the first two tasks during the second half of the due diligence timeframe. This allows to include the plans and risks of the new entity and of the merger integration into the decision to acquire. The execution of the merger integration project is often started before close (as an internal project within the acquirer organization) with a later inclusion of the target people after close.

Timing is important for these tasks. In my opinion, *Design the new entity* and *Plan Merger Integration* have to happen as early as possible, even within the due diligence phase.

Design of the new entity

Design of the new entity is a task within merger integration that should be carried out as early as possible in the M&A process. Here we propose to do this during due diligence. The obvious goal of merger integration is to create a new entity leveraging the existing organizations of acquirer and target.

Typical objectives are:

❏ Business continuity: this is a goal in widespread use in merger integrations. You have to make sure you do not disrupt business in the acquirer and in the target. In the software industry this can mean that you continue to sell products via the target and that you start selling the target products via the acquiring entity.

❏ Completeness: you have to integrate all parts of the target as planned in the business case, covering all layers of the enterprise architecture.

❏ Coverage of all layers: you have to cover all aspects of a business system, spanning all layers of the enterprise architecture. While the resource layer is taken care of in all merger integrations and the business process layer is taken care of in most integrations, the business strategy and business plan layer is not taken care of in all integrations. The recommendation here is to take care of all layers equally.

Design the new entity

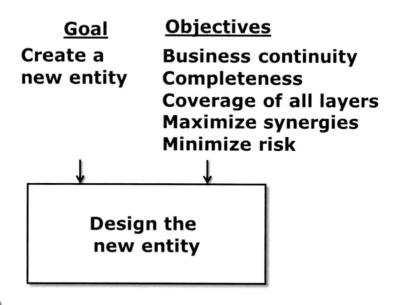

© Dr. Karl Popp 2013

Figure 25: Design the new entity

❑ Minimize risk of failure: many post merger integrations fail. This is why you have to create the new entity in a way that minimizes risk of failure, e.g. by planning merger integration already in due diligence.

❑ Maximize synergies: one measure of business performance is taking care of realizing the synergies that are planned for the merger integration. Maximizing synergies can mean that the entities are integrated quickly or slowly, depending on the specific synergies planned.

This calls for a definition of synergies. Synergies are goals and objectives for post merger integration that often relate to changes of employment, lowering cost or increasing revenue during or after the post merger integration.

Example

> *Examples for usual synergies in post merger integrations are cost objectives, which occur due to integration of administrative functions of both companies. Another example are revenue objectives, e.g. since target's and acquirer's products can be sold to more customers.*

Based on the enterprise architecture we can create a view of synergies that has higher precision and completeness.

Synergies can be modeled on the business strategy and plan layer, but can also be broken down into the business process model and resources layer. A synergy model is a interaction model, with synergies assigned to objects and/or relationships. A synergy model is complete if each object and relationship has at least one synergy goal or synergy objective assigned.

3.3   Characteristics of M&A transactions

To improve understanding of M&A transactions, let us have a look at characteristics of these transactions. This will help us improve the due diligence and management of M&A transactions overall.

Business dynamics of target and acquirer

Structural and behavioral dynamics apply for both, the acquiring and the acquired entity as well as the environment of both companies.

Using an interaction diagram, we can already identify potential dynamics as follows. We look at each of the objects and each of the relationships to identify dynamics.

By looking at the interaction diagram and all potential dynamics of all transactions, you get closer to a complete model of dynamics of a business system (from an outside view).

Interaction model of the Business Strategy and business plan layer

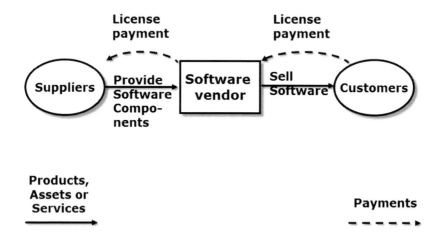

Figure 26: Dynamics of M&A transactions

A special case of dynamics is strategy dynamics, which we have discussed before.

Example

Let us have a look at some dynamics of selected objects and transactions between the supplier and the software vendor from Figure 26.

Suppliers: Suppliers might change their strategy, their behavior or the supplier market undergoes dramatic changes, maybe again by several suppliers merging or by a supplier getting acquired by a competitor of the software vendor. Another change might be that a supplier goes out of business.

Provide software components: the supplier might be providing the software components as usual or late or never due to going out of business. The supplier might change its release strategy.

License payment: the supplier might raise prices of the supplied software components. Or the supplier might change the business model of the contract to a bulk payment on the next renewal of the contract.

Time lags also play an important role, since the integration of both companies does not take place instantly. This influences the speed of creating synergies of the merger integration.

More detail for acquisition transactions

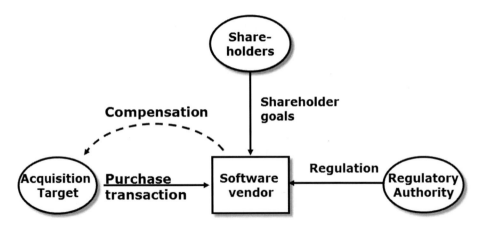

© Dr. Karl Popp 2012

Figure 27: Sources of deal dynamics

Foundations of mergers and acquisitions

Deal dynamics

The transaction itself carries dynamics, which we can identify looking at a more detailed interaction diagram of the acquisition transactions taking place (Figure 27).

Each of the external objects involved (shareholders, regulatory authorities and acquisition targets) can change their behavior and might be in favor of the transactions or not. If one of the involved external objects is not in favor, additional complexity and effort is added to the transaction to persuade or to force external objects to be in favor of the transaction.

External factors and obstacles

There are numerous obstacles for merger integration inside and outside of the involved entities, which might create time lags in synergy creation and in rare cases they might prevent the acquisition as well as the merger integration.

Typical examples are interactions and decision processes involving workers councils as well as external impact from tax and regulatory authorities. In addition, shareholders can be a source of obstacles to the deal (Figure 27), e.g. if they are not approving the purchase.

The number of and the influence of external factors depends on the territory (countries) where the merger takes place. This is why an international merger has additional complexity from the external factors existent in the countries and their regulatory authorities involved in the merger integration.

Complexity of the target and of merger integration

Let us look again at a complexity model, which was in part presented earlier in this book. The model is used to determine the effort of the post merger integration based on the complexity of the merger integration project.

In addition to what we learned earlier, we are adding the following to the complexity model:

❑ The dimension "restructuring" which takes into account the changes to be made during the integration

❑ Information about the acquiring company in the dimension volume.

Complexity of merger integration

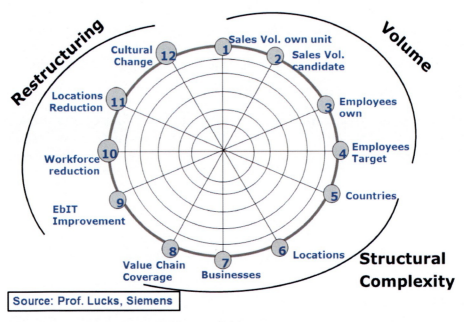

Source: Prof. Lucks, Siemens

Figure 28: A complexity model for acquisitions

The resulting complexity model is shown in Figure 28.

Before we look at completeness of this complexity model, let us have a look at two examples.

Example

Company A is a medium size software vendor and Company B is a is a large software vendor. This example is based on anonymized real companies.

Complexity of business systems: Examples

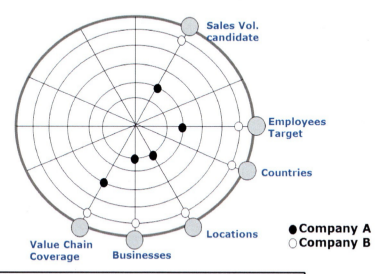

Source: Chart: Prof. Lucks, Siemens, Examples: Dr. Karl Popp

Figure 29: Examples of complexity models for acquisitions

In a corresponding chart for these two acquisitions, we clearly see different values in each of the dimensions. The idea is to get a notion of the complexity of the post merger integration, by taking the area covered by the graph that connects all the data points. In Figure 29 you see that the area covered by the Company B graph is bigger than the Company A graph leading to the assumption that the complexity and effort of the Company B integration might be bigger than the complexity and effort of the Company A integration.

3.4   M&A Processes

An M&A Process is a business process model defining the tasks, the involved roles and the execution sequence of the tasks to analyze the purchase, to decide the purchase and to integrate the acquired assets or companies. Another aspect is project management. For this aspect, we propose to involve certified project management professionals.

Mergers and acquisitions are conducted following the M&A process. Although there are many different definitions of the M&A process, there are a few basic similarities between these, which we will show here first. As stated before, all activities serve one purpose: the decision to acquire and if acquired, to execute the integration.

M&A process maturity model

Here, we build on the capability maturity model integration (CMMI®) (CMMI_Product_Team, 2010) and look at the capability of the receiving organization and at the maturity of the M&A process. For full details, please see the documentation (CMMI_Product_Team, 2010).

For successful M&A processes, we propose to reach at least level 3 for capability and maturity as a prerequisite for successful M&A execution. This means that all processes for M&A execution are defined and can be tailored for a specific M&A project.

Organizations having a lower level of capability and maturity than level 3 run a significant process risk in the M&A process. They might forget activities or badly execute activities in critical phases of the M&A process and thus endanger the success of the transaction.

M&A process capability and maturity

| Capability |

0 – *Incomplete:* Goals are not reached.

| Maturity |

1 – *Performed:* The goals are reached.

1 – *Initial* : No requirements, usually ad hoc processes.

2 – *Managed* The process is executed, monitored, controlled and reviewed.

2 – *Managed:* processes are planned, executed and can be repeated.

3 – *Defined* Process is tailored from an existing process definition for execution.

3 – *Defined:* Standards, methods, processes and tools are defined. Specific processes are tailored.

4 – *Quantitatively managed:* Quantitative objectives are defined and measured.

| Source: CMMI® for development, Version 1.3 |

5 – *Optimizing*: Ongoing improvement happens based on process statistics.

Figure 30: Process capability and maturity for M&A processes

A simplified M&A process

Let us start with a simplified process to understand the basics about what happens in an M&A process. After presenting the assumptions, we will provide an overview of the process steps.

Basic assumptions

For simplification, let us assume the following

❐ we only have one target company;

❐ it is a share deal with cash compensation;

❐ the acquiring company has an executive board and the executive board takes all acquisition related decisions,

Foundations of mergers and acquisitions

- ☐ budget for the acquisition is available,
- ☐ It is a friendly acquisition,
- ☐ The acquisition target is private company,
- ☐ There is no competitive offer and no bidding competition.
- ☐ This is not a distressed target sale.

By using these assumptions, we can look at a process that fits many acquisitions and shows the core elements of an M&A process. We will later drop the assumptions to see what happens to our simplified process.

Simplified M&A process

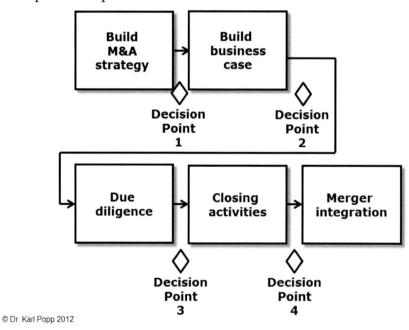

© Dr. Karl Popp 2012

Figure 31: A simple M&A process

Foundations of mergers and acquisitions

Build M&A strategy and decision proposal

First, a company identifies the need to acquire, then it formulates the intent to acquire and may select a target from a shortlist of potential targets. The decision about continuing the process is prepared. This might happen in several iternations. The decision proposal usually contains information about the strategy, public information about the target and about a potential price range for the target. Since M&A strategy is not the subject of this book, we point to (Smith, 2012) for more background information. The usual information needed is: market size, desired market share, estimated target value and purchase price, aspired cost and revenue synergies, product fit with own products, aspired product roadmap and integration with own products.

Decision point 1

The executive board decides if the process continues or not. This already is an investment decision, since dedicated M&A resources will work in this process.

Build the business case

Resources are assigned to work on creating the business case. With just one target, a business case document for the acquisition is built and presented to the executive board. This document contains a rough business plan, product strategy and roadmap for acquired products and services and a draft valuation model based on estimated cost and revenue.

In parallel, the negotiation team works with the target company to determine if the target would like to sell.

Decision point 2

Then the decision is taken to go ahead and start a formal acquisition process, often with a letter of intent exchanged between acquirer and target. So the board decides to issue a letter of intent and approves the acquisition related cost that occur in the following due diligence phase, like travel cost, cost for external auditors etc.

Run due diligence

The next step is the due diligence, which serves the following purposes:

- ❑ to collect information about the target and to validate assumptions. With a focus on merger integration, this phase contains mandatory tasks like commercial due diligence, HR and cultural due diligence and drafting an integration plan and schedule.

- ❑ To surface any risk associated with the acquisition and integration and to identify significant risks that would lead to failure of the business plan or of the integration (deal breakers).

- ❑ To create a draft post merger integration plan and to evaluate it.

- ❑ To summarize and aggregate the results of the due diligence for the decision to acquire.

- ❑ A due diligence report is created containing all the information mentioned above.

Decision point 2: Decision to acquire and signing

When due diligence has been completed, the decision to acquire is taken by the acquirer based on the information collected in the due diligence phase. With a focus on merger integration, a key input to this decision is the integration plan.

Closing activities

At the beginning of this process step, the acquisition contract is signed. One section of the contract usually lists the closing tasks to be carried out by the target. So the next step in the closing activities is that the target executes these tasks.

If approvals from regulatory authorities is needed, these approvals are being collected.

If all closing conditions are met and all closing tasks have been successfully executed, the deal closes.

Foundations of mergers and acquisitions

Definition of merger

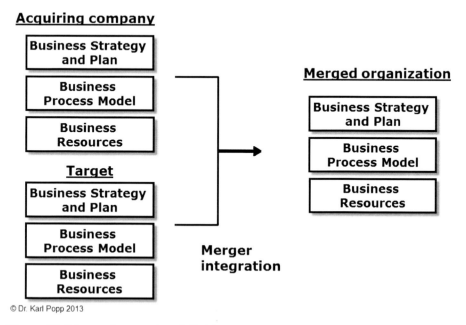

© Dr. Karl Popp 2013

Figure 32: Merger integration definition

Merger integration

As mentioned before, in merger integration the target and acquiring organization and processes are integrated. The draft plan for merger integration, that was created in the process step *Due diligence* is reviewed and amended first thing in Merger integration. After that, the merger integration plan is executed.

Process impact of giving up assumptions

Now that we understood the simplified process, let us take a look what happens if we give up one of the assumptions.

Impact of having several potential targets

If there are several potential targets, the process step "Build M&A strategy and decision proposal" is expanded to contain the process for selecting a target. Several targets undergo a preliminary analysis and the targets are compared using pros and cons. One of the targets is selected. The rest of the process remains unchanged.

Impact of an asset deal

If just assets are acquired, these assets are transferred from the target to the acquirer. Since you basically carve out the assets you have to make sure you do not loose or you do replace existing connections of the assets like employment contracts, supplier relationships and customer contracts. You also should make sure that there are no more dependencies from the acquired assets to the assets remaining at the target.

Example

A software vendor acquires two products and hires the corresponding development teams. It is important to ensure that the development teams can continue their development work and that the acquired products do no more depend on assets that are still with the target.

So the impact of an asset deal on the M&A process is, that there are additional efforts to ensure completeness and independency of assets and that the business surrounding the assets can be continued. For most asset deals, the overall process is usually simpler than the process for a share deal.

Impact of non-cash compensation

If the assumption of cash compensation is removed, a compensation in equity or other matter is used. An equity compensation means that the owners of the target get an equity stake in exchange of the ownership rights in the target company. For the owners of the target, this introduces a value risk, since the value of the equity compensation can vary over time.

Budget for the transaction is not available

If financing is needed, the process step "Build M&A strategy and decision proposal" is expanded to establish e.g. a credit line or financing for the transaction. When the deal is signed, the credit line or the financing is used to pay the purchase price (mostly in parts, retaining a certain percentage to cover undiscovered liabilities and risks).

Hostile acquisition

A hostile acquisition means that a target is being acquired by a competitor. The goal for such an acquisition is often consolidation of markets. Hostile acquisitions have higher than normal risk of:

❒ losing key people due to layoffs in consolidation efforts and

❒ of executing consolidation efforts, like resolving products overlaps in product portfolio consolidations.

The process impact of hostile acquisitions is that there is usually little to no due diligence done on the target (since the target does not want to reveal details to competition) and that there are higher efforts for consolidation due to overlaps in corporate functions and development and support organizations.

Public company

If the target is a public company, there are several process changes. Since the target is a public company, the visibility of the transaction to the public is much higher than for a private company. Shareholders of the target will protect their interest by demanding a fair share price to be paid and by demanding that the target's business remains undisturbed until the transaction is closed.

One process change is that there cannot be a joint merger integration planning in the due diligence phase. In addition, the information disclosed by the target in the due diligence phase might be less than the information you get in due diligence for a private company.

The process to get share from all shareholders might take a long time depending on the local laws for acquisitions of publicly traded companies.

Bidding competition

If several bidders exist for a target, a bidding competition might happen. For the process a bidding competition means that the "Build M&A strategy and decision proposal" is expanded to serve the bidding iterations until the bidding competition is over or the maximum price the acquiring company wants to pay is reached.

3.5   M&A organization

How do organizations best prepare for running M&A processes? How do they organize to be successful? What are the challenges? Which and how many resources are working on M&A? Let us see which questions we can answer here.

Typical roles and teams working on M&A

Looking at the roles and teams involved in M&A processes in different companies, the following seems to be a popular set of roles involved in mergers and acquisitions. In small companies, one person might be covering several roles, while in large companies some of the roles might be done by teams of people.

Executive sponsor

The executive sponsor is the CEO, managing director or a member of the executive board of the acquiring company.

Business owner

The business owner is an executive, who runs the business, where the target organization will be integrated.

Negotiation team

The negotiation team consists of one or more experienced negotiators who are acquainted with deal structures and with acquisition contracts as well as negotiation strategies.

Valuation experts

Valuation experts are educated financial modelers. They create a financial model of the acquired company and of the deal as an investment.

Experts on administration functions

Experts from different organizations of the acquiring company are needed to evaluate and to integrate the target. These experts come from functions like IT, controlling, finance.

Product and production experts

In the software industry, product experts are needed to evaluate the software products of the target. They come from development, product management or solution management and from quality assurance.

M&A organizational maturity model

I am proposing an organizational maturity model that has three dimensions: M&A experience, number of corporate functions existing and number of dedicated M&A personnel. The first dimension is M&A experience. M&A experience has proven to be of utmost importance for successful M&A deals. Experience of managers covers the number of deals that managers involved have gone through, especially dealing with exceptional situations and change management. To become more independent on the experience of specific people, each company should install

M&A experience management to make sure to store and reuse the experiences made.

Organizational maturity model for M&A

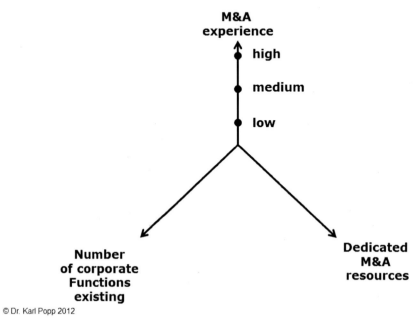

© Dr. Karl Popp 2012

Figure 33: Organization maturity model

M&A organization in small companies

In small companies, there usually is the managing director driving M&A processes. This is a heavy duty for him, so he often looks for help and advice and hires an outside counsel and maybe an M&A advisory firm.

Organizational maturity model for small companies

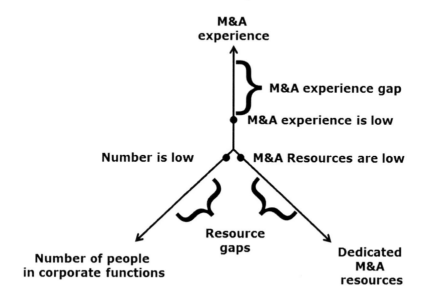

© Dr. Karl Popp 2012

Figure 34: Organization maturity for small companies

The challenges

Challenges for small companies are in analysing the opportunity, in running the due diligence right and in executing the post merger integration with severe resource bottlenecks. The managing director and maybe the CFO are spending most of their workday on activities in the M&A project. This might lead to severe impact on day-to-day business and is a key risk in M&A projects for small companies.

Example

Here is a citation from the due diligence of a small software vendor. The CEO said: "This due diligence is an efficient way to shut down our company. All management seems to be working on due diligence tasks."

The solution

As mentioned before, it is important for the acquiring company to continue business. This is only possible if key players of the acquiring company are not fully covered by acquisition related tasks. So hiring outside M&A advisors and consultants helping corporate functions to execute due diligence and integration work is highly advised.

M&A organization in medium sized companies

In medium sized companies, we have more organizational structure than in small companies and explicit corporate functions with limited headcount. Opportunities for acquisitions are mostly analyzed by business development or business strategy departments.

The decision is taken by the managing director or board of directors, while the integration execution lays in the hands of a project manager, mostly picked from finance or business development.

The challenges

Challenges are limited experience, high strain on executive resources due to M&A tasks and resource bottlenecks in the integration phase.

Organizational maturity model for medium sized companies

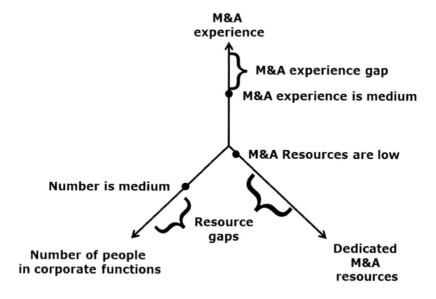

© Dr. Karl Popp 2012

Figure 35: Organization maturity for medium sized companies

The solution

Although there is a larger organization than in small companies, medium sized companies should consider help from outside of the company for acquisition and merger integration. So sometimes M&A advisory firms help in the due diligence and the integration process.

M&A organization in large companies

In large companies we find specialized functions for business development and business strategy, sometimes also explicit headcount and departments for mergers and acquisitions. If there is a central team for M&A, this team usually is responsible for analyzing, coordinating, negotiating or valuating M&A opportunities.

The challenges

Large companies are challenged by their size (and sometimes also by the size of their target companies). During merger integration, coordination of all the corporate functions and of the overall integration project are paramount. Administrative corporate functions are overloaded by merger work if not appropriately staffed.

Organizational maturity model for large companies

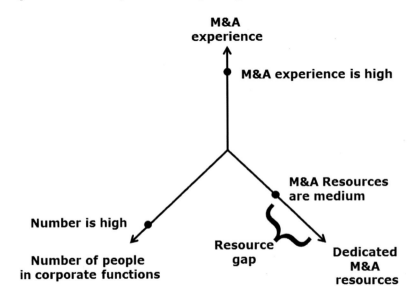

© Dr. Karl Popp 2012

Figure 36: Organization maturity for large companies

The solution

Leveraging the M&A experience and ongoing process improvements, large companies should be well prepared for due diligence of targets. For merger integration, they profit from engaging certified project management professionals to manage a large and complex merger integration project. Dedicated M&A functions help in the projects and in addition, resource bottlenecks are covered by outside consultants.

Recommendation

I would recommend to work with Osborne Clarke as they are industry experts and know the legal and tax requirements of (international) M&A in the Digital Business sector, especially in the software industry, inside out. They give real practical advice from their vast experience, all with an unstuffy approach.

3.6 Patterns in developing M&A organizations in frequent acquirers

How do firms organize, that frequently acquire other companies? How does organization and process evolve over time? Let us look at a typical evolution of M&A organization and processes over time. I see basically four steps happening.

Step 1: Get and centralize M&A knowledge and experience

Starting to acquire companies, firms often do not have experienced, dedicated resources for M&A. So they hire employees or hire consultants with M&A knowledge. The organization uses this knowledge but is usually not well equipped with enough resources and hardly anyone in the organization has run M&A processes before.

As mentioned before, installing a practice and processes for M&A experience management is paramount.

Step 2: Get the process right

So the next phase is that companies focus on process and process education and documentation of company specific processes and tasks in merger integration. Still they lack resources for such exceptional work effort resulting from the merger integration tasks.

Step 3: Get buffer resources in place for central functions

So companies tend to build centralized buffer resources and a specialized M&A function to cover merger integration efforts. This M&A function provides guidance on processes, experiences and best practices from earlier acquisitions and merger integrations.

Step 4: Decide if central or decentral or hybrid approach

After the evolutionary steps outlined above, corporate functions create M&A departments inside corporate functions, like e.g. an M&A finance function as part of corporate finance. Coordination of merger integration projects is done by a central team. Or a company might decide to put M&A functions in each of its divisions. The idea behind that is that the divisions know their business best and will figure out how to be successful. Which approach, central or decentral, suits a company best is a tricky question. We can get closer to an answer, if we look at advantages and disadvantages of central and decentral approach to M&A:

Central approach advantages

❑ Good knowledge sharing and central storage for best practices.

❑ Full time resources are available and not impacted by resource constraints in the functional areas of the company.

Central approach disadvantages

❑ Distance to business: central teams are neither integrated into day-to-day business operations nor into corporate functions.

❑ Potential conflict on competences, responsibilities and accountabilities: basically the intrinsic issues of a matrix organization apply here: the central M&A Team and the division receiving the target organization might be in conflict.

Decentral approach pros

❏ Competences, responsibilities and accountabilities reside in the business, not the central team.

❏ Management and control of the merger integration project is within the business.

Decentral approach cons

❏ Low central knowledge sharing and central storage for best practices. As explained below, this can be overcome by establishing a knowledge sharing community.

❏ Resource constraints might have an impact on the merger integration success. Depending on the frequency of acquisitions, the decentral teams might have enough resources or not.

❏ Centralized experience and best practices management is challenging.

Hybrid approach

So to balance the pros and cons listed here, some large corporations have installed a hybrid M&A organization: central teams that are collecting and sharing M&A knowledge and supporting the decentral team as well as coaching for M&A projects, while the merger integration is executed by decentral teams.

Example

Siemens, a frequent acquirer, has a hybrid approach. While a central team assures guidance and support, the M&A integration is carried out by the different divisions, which have their own M&A teams, caring for due diligence and post merger integration.

3.7   Takeaways from chapter 3

We have looked at definitions as well as transactions and deal types. We defined merger integration and merger integration tasks, which allow to prepare better for merger integration already in due diligence. Then we tried to elaborate on the characteristics of M&A transactions in general which prepares us for real life in M&A and merger integration. After defining a general, simplified M&A process, we extended this process for several real world situations, which allows us to select the right process for a specific M&A situation.

Looking at organizations for M&A, we saw that there are different shapes and sizes of organizations and learned about the pros and cons of these ways to organize for M&A and ended this chapter with looking at patterns in frequent acquirers.This lays the foundation for further discussions in this book and also for better coping with mergers and acquisitions in your professional life.

DRKARLPOPP.COM M&A videos

Based on this book, i have created videos on due diligence, post merger integration, risk management, IP management and many other topics. many more. The objective is to provide software business education for software executives online at
http://www.drkarlpopp.com/softwareecosystemvideos.html .

Education using videos is cheap, convenient and effective. Please use the link below to access the videos. Try them today! You can find my M&A education videos on
http://www.udemy.com/ma-mergers-and-acquisitions-basics/.

4. Foundations of due diligence

When acquiring a company you deal with uncertainty and information asymmetry. Be aware that uncertainty and information asymmetry exist between your company and your target, but also within your company, between different people and organizations. You need well researched information to take an informed decision if you should acquire or not.

Having read this chapter, you will have basic knowledge of due diligence, due diligence tasks, the different types of due diligence and their pros and cons. Let us have a look at the task "Due diligence" on a very high level first.

© Dr. Karl Popp 2012

Figure 37: Goals and objectives of due diligence

4.1 The goals and objectives of due diligence

The goal of due diligence activities is to provide information for an informed decision to buy a company. Objectives measure business performance, meaning how well the goals are achieved. Figure 37 gives an overview. In line with the focus of this book, one key objective is to maximize the likelihood of integration success.

Now let us look into the exact meaning of the presented goal of due diligence.

Goal: Providing information for an informed decision

Providing information on one hand means that the acquiring company collects information about the target. This information can come from the target and other sources that can provide information about the target and its ecosystem. Information collecting can be, and often is, outsourced to specialized information collection experts like auditors and legal advisors.

Providing information on the other hand means that the merger integration that would follow an acquisition is planned preliminarily and these plan is being evaluated. For the target, the business is modeled and analysed and risks are modeled. For the merger integration, the merged entity is designed and risks and synergies of the merged entity and of the merger integration are modeled.

In addition, *providing information* means that the information is aggregated and presented. So shaping the information is paramount. The result of due diligence is often called the due diligence report and contains condensed results from many different due diligence activities rolled into one.

To serve the objective *minimize risk*, providing information about risk by identifying and evaluating risk is also included here.

A due diligence report can be pretty generic and able to serve a number of potential buyers and a number of involved roles like CEO, CFO, lawyers and auditors.

Due diligence goal and actions

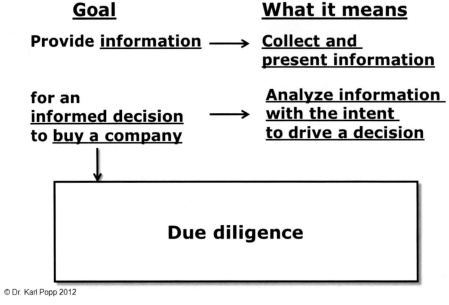

© Dr. Karl Popp 2012

Figure 38: Goals and actions of due diligence

Analyse information with the intent to drive a decision

Results from the information collection and presentation are supposed to give you appropriate information about the status of the acquired company or assets as well as of the merger integration and its synergies and risks. But to take a decision, the information has to be prepared to be able to take a decision.

Often, this preparation means aggregations, omissions, focusing on material issues and deal brakers and plans for the overall deal and integration. But aggregation and omissions carry the risk of creating a wrong picture.

Objectives and ways to reach the objectives

In addition to goals, the corresponding objectives help you to reach the most favourable result out of the many possible results. Here are exemplary ways to reach the objectives of the due diligence task in the software industry as defined in Figure 37.

Due diligence objectives

Objectives	Ways to reach them (examples)
Minimize information asymmetry	Get additional information via third party service providers like Open Source scans, Security scans of the software to be acquired
Minimize risk	Being aware of generic risks of M&A, analysing the risk of the deal based on a risk catalogue, review risks and impact of past M&A processes
Maximize quality of results	High capability maturity level, leverage internal experts as reviewers of results
Maximize likelihood of integration success	Plan carefully, use internal experts for reviews for the plan, review risks and impact of past integration plans and results

© Dr. Karl Popp 2012

Figure 39: Due diligence objectives

4.2   The decision to acquire

While generic due diligence results can be used by many potential buyers, the decision to acquire is always specific to the current situation of the acquiring company. The decision to acquire is a decision task that the management of the acquiring company has to execute.

The decision to acquire is a decision under uncertainty. While we have tried to minimize the uncertainty in due diligence, there is still enough uncertainty left. The uncertainty relates to the following topics, which are amended with example questions about the uncertainties like:

☐ the information available from the target: is it complete, is it accurate?

☐ The business plan for the acquisition: is it complete, is it consistent? What is the best case and the worst case outcome?

☐ The integration plan: is it realistic? Is the receiving organization and the target capable to execute? Are the involved integration managers capable of managing the integration properly?

☐ The assumptions of the acquisition about the target, the suppliers, the customers, the competitors, the receiving organization, the integration plan: are they realistic? Are they time dependent? What happens if we give up an assumption?

4.3 Decomposing the due diligence tasks

In due diligence, we provide information about two things: the target and the merger integration. So the task *Due Diligence* is decomposed accordingly:

Target due diligence analyzes the status quo of the target from many perspectives like financials, controlling, human resources etc.

Merger integration due diligence defines merger integration plans, evaluates these merger integration plans and summarizes the results for the decision to acquire.

Decomposing the due diligence task

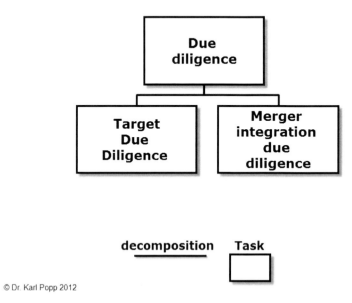

© Dr. Karl Popp 2012

Figure 40: Decomposing the due diligence task

4.4　Classic types of Due diligence activities

Based on the enterprise architecture, let us look at due diligence activities and how they are aggregated to different types of due diligence activities. We will also map the classical types of due diligence activities to the enterprise architecture.

Strategic due diligence

In strategy due diligence we verify or falsify hypotheses that are related to the strategy model on level 1 of the enterprise architecture. Usually the classic approach covers the existing strategy, no matter if it is complete or not. In our approach we can first check if the strategy is complete and then analyse.

Market due diligence

In market due diligence we check hypotheses regarding sets of instances of external objects in the interaction diagram on level 1 of the enterprise architecture. These can be customers, suppliers, partners, employees but also legal authorities. In classic due diligence the markets are analysed that the target or the acquirer sees. In our approach we see all external objects in the interaction model in the business strategy and plan layer as potential markets. By doing that, we can make sure we strive for complete coverage of markets.

Commercial due diligence

In commercial due diligence we check hypotheses regarding the business model and the external relationships of the target. This due diligence type often contains the so-called operations due diligence, where the operations model is reviewed and evaluated.

Technical due diligence

Technical due diligence looks at technical resources on level 3 of the enterprise architecture. These can be all technical resources like machines, production sites or technical intellectual property. In the software industry the focus is usually on intellectual property and technical due diligence of the software products regarding e.g. architecture and quality attributes of the software products. While you would like to avoid to look at the source code, you need to get detail information about it. This is why you should hire service providers to do a code inspection. I recommend Hartings GmbH from Düsseldorf, Germany for code inspection services.

Human resources due diligence

In human resources due diligence we check hypotheses regarding employees and managers on level 3 of the enterprise architecture.

Cultural due diligence

Cultural due diligence happens on the resource level and looks at the company culture. It is often contained in human resources due diligence.

Intellectual property due diligence

Intellectual property due diligence reviews the IP resources on level 3 and also looks at the processes on level 2 of the enterprise architecture. In focus are creation and documentation of intellectual property, protection of IP and compliance with licenses for third party IP. We will go into more detail in a later chapter in this book.

Financial due diligence

Financial due diligence looks at financial resources and all processes which make use of, control and monitor financial resources.

Tax due diligence

In tax due diligence we verify hypotheses regarding the payments to tax authorities that the target has done.

Besides the classic types of due diligence, we propose to do merger integration due diligence in addition.

4.5   Critical examination of due diligence types and their frequency

Now that we know the different types of due diligence, how and how often are these different types used in acquisition processes? In a study by Gerds (Gerds 2010) we find information how often the different types are used. He looked at numerous German companies and came up with the following findings.

Histogram of typical due diligence exercises

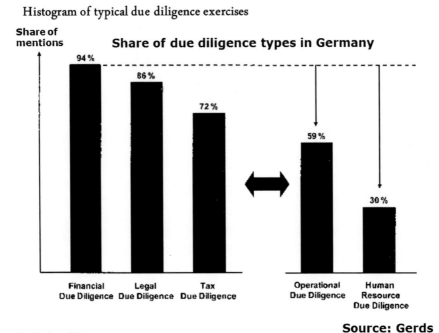

© Dr. Karl Popp 2013

Figure 41: Histogram of due diligence types in acquisition processes (Gerds 2010)

While financial, legal and tax due diligence are executed in most, but not all transactions, operational due diligence and HR due diligence are underrepresented. To find out if this a good or a bad situation, Gerds provides a look at anticipated risks of an acquisition and how the risks map to the types of due diligence. It shows how often risks were anticipated in the study and how often different due diligence types were named, too.

Looking at financial due diligence and how often finance risks were named, we can interpret the study that the participants of the study take good care of financial risk. Legal and tax due diligence seem to cover corresponding risks also well.

Anticipated risk and typical due diligence exercises

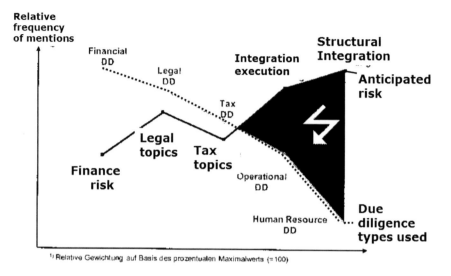

Source: Gerds

Figure 42: Risk and due diligence types (Gerds 2010)

The situation is different when we look at operational and HR due diligence. Here, corresponding risks for integration execution and structural integration are named very often. And while many participants of the study see these risks, operational due diligence and HR due diligence are less popular than the corresponding anticipated risks. This is especially important for the task of merger integration.

This gap has to be overcome, especially in the light of a knowledge intensive industry like the software industry, which is highly dependent on its employees. The solution is simple, HR due diligence should be an integral part of each due diligence in the software industry. To properly cover integration execution risk, we propose to perform merger integration due diligence.

4.6   Due diligence as a modeling activity

Let us have a look at coverage of existing due diligence activities regarding the enterprise architecture, meaning which due diligence activities relate to which level of the Enterprise architecture.

Mapping of typical due diligence exercises to the Enterprise architecture

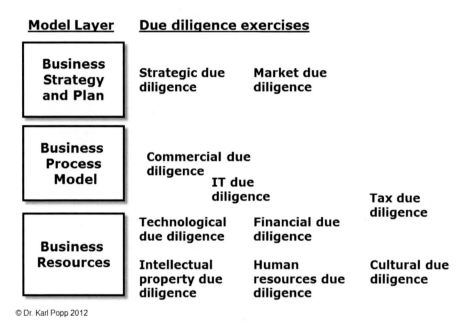

© Dr. Karl Popp 2012

Figure 43: Mapping of due diligence types to layers

We do this to make sure that all parts of the enterprise are covered by the classic types of due diligence activities.

Looking at Figure 43, we see that many due diligence types are related to the resource layer and few to the business process and business strategy layer. This is a good approach to model the status quo of the company at a certain point of time, but it has a weak spot regarding potential and strategy of a target.

Inherent challenges of due diligence activities

Since due diligence is a complex task and you have to deal with uncertain and missing information and with two entities, the acquirer and the target, there are numerous inherent challenges of due diligence activities:

☐ Challenges to get valid information about the status quo,

☐ Challenges of modeling the status quo,

☐ Management of complexity of the situation,

☐ Management of dependencies between the models,

☐ Dynamics of change,

☐ Lack of time,

☐ Lack of data,

☐ Lots of risk everywhere.

Let us walk through these challenges step by step:

Challenges to get valid information about the status quo

Information about a target company can be correct. But it may not be. Information about a target company can be wrong. But you may have no way to tell so. So the question arises why it is so difficult to get information about the target, which is correct and available on time when it is needed. As we will see, there are several intrinsic problems in the way we usually do due diligence.

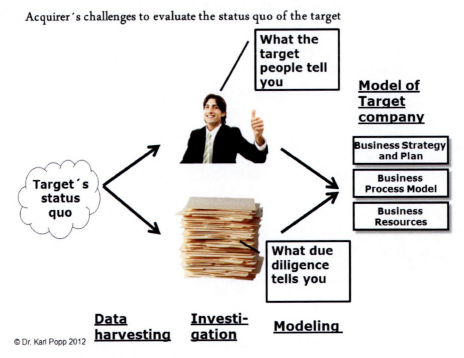

Figure 44: Challenges to acquire information

Challenges of modeling the status quo

As in every modeling activity, the model differs from reality. All due diligence models, from financial to tax due diligence suffer from this. It is of paramount importance to make sure you understand the differences and that you document the assumptions, omissions and simplifications present in your due diligence models. This will help you understand the limitations of due diligence result much better.

Modeling challenges of due diligence

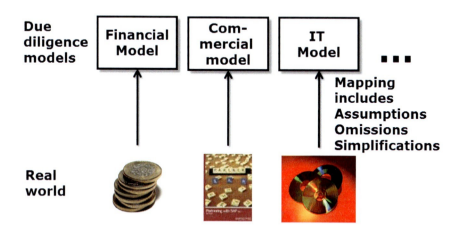

© Dr. Karl Popp 2012

Figure 45: Status quo modeling challenges in due diligence

To make things worse, the real world you would like to model might be fuzzy, you might not have detail knowledge or you have no knowledge and then you have to work based on assumptions only. This is one of the key problems in due diligence: to get a fair model of the status quo. At the same time, it is a key problem in post merger integration, because you cannot integrate well what you do not know well enough.

A good starting point is to know about the fuzziness of due diligence models and to manage the assumptions.

Management of the complexity of the situation

We learned about complexity measures in section "Complexity of business systems" in this book. Generally speaking, due diligence complexity rises with the complexity of the target and the complexity of the receiving entity. Imagine a company that has three businesses, 20.000 employees and operates with subsidiaries in seven countries.

To manage that complexity is one of the big challenges and risks of merger integration. One way to cope with complexity is to define complexity using the complexity model proposed in this book and to plan tasks and resources according to that complexity.

Management of dependencies

There are many dependencies within the target and within the merger integration plan that have to be analysed and reflected in planning and change management. While there are typically separate due diligence tracks run on financials, tax, product due diligence you have to make sure these tracks are in synch to reflect the dependencies between these tracks.

One way to cope with dependencies is to make them explicit. Frequent successful acquirers know the dependencies between different due diligence and merger integration activities, make them explicit and manage them accordingly.

Examples

Here are examples for dependencies: The revenue plan depends on the availability dates of products. The availability dates of products depend on development plans. If development plans slip, revenue plans slip as well.

The dates of legal merge of target subsidiaries with the subsidiaries of the acquiring company depend on tax planning. If the tax planning and the dates for legal merge change, dates for all dependent measures like transferring support relationships from the target to the acquirer and availability of products from the target pricelist gets prolonged etc.

Dynamics of change

Changes happen always and everywhere. Models and assumptions are based on a snapshot of the real world. So if you create a financial model, a commercial model and an IT model in due diligence, these models might have been built at different moments in time.

Business System dynamics as a challenge for due diligence

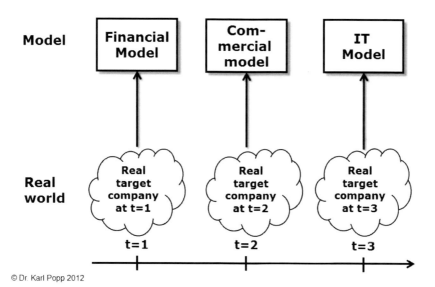

© Dr. Karl Popp 2012

Figure 46: Dynamics as a challenge for due diligence

But changes are also happening in the acquiring company during the M&A process. Strategies and organization may change for example right after the signing of the deal. Strategies and plans for the M&A project would have to be adapted or overhauled. In due diligence you can cope with these dynamics by establishing regular synch points between the different due diligence tracks.

Foundations of due diligence

4.7 Merger integration due diligence

We introduce merger integration due diligence as a new type of due diligence that arises from the objective "Maximize likelihood of integration success" that was introduced earlier in this book. Since merger integrations have a high likelihood to fail, a review of merger integration plans and merger integration projects is paramount. So let us define what merger integration due diligence is.

Definition of Merger Integration Due Diligence

Merger integration due diligence has the goal to review the merger integration project and plans.

Merger integration due diligence task

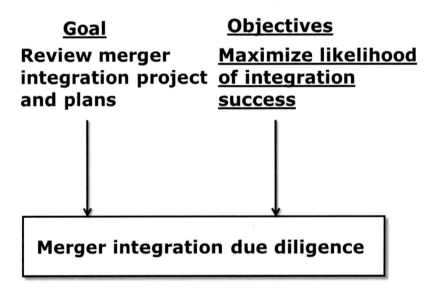

© Dr. Karl Popp 2013

Figure 47: Merger integration due diligence task

So all aspects of merger integration are being reviewed for viability and for likelihood of success. Viability relates to the work breakdown structure for the integration to be consistent and complete. It also relates to resources (employees and budgets) that have to be sufficient and available. The objective of the task is to maximize the likelihood of merger integration success.

Based on the decomposition of the merger integration task we can define the corresponding decomposition of the merger integration due diligence task.

Decomposing the merger integration due diligence task

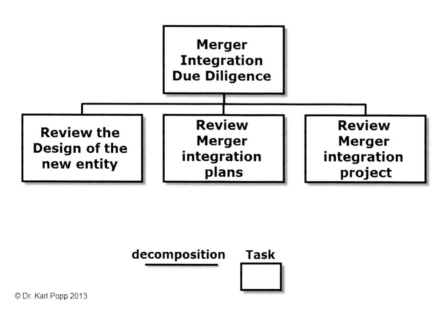

© Dr. Karl Popp 2013

Figure 48: Merger integration due diligence task decomposition

Review of the design of the new entity

The design of the new entity has to be reviewed for consistency and completeness. In the approach proposed in this book, the structure and behavior of the new entity as defined along the enterprise architecture is reviewed. We start with the business strategy and plan layer and review the defined business strategy for the new entity. Then we enter the second layer and review the structure and behavior of the new entity with questions like: will the business processes work? Are the business processes compliant with compliance rules? Is governance of the business ensured?

In parallel, we have a look at the business resources and at the questions: Are enough qualified resources planned and available? Are the assignments of resources to tasks sufficient? Are sufficient resources planned and available?

Review merger integration plans

Next we review merger integration plans. Keeping in mind the design of the new entity and the resource situation, we review the schedules and the steps of the merger integration plans. We ask questions like: Can the merger integration plan be executed the way it is defined? Will sufficient resources and budgets be available at the right time to execute the merger integration plan successfully? What happens if we run late or we have resource shortages?

Review merger integration project

This is the part of the review that is often neglected in practice. We review the structure and behavior of the merger integration project.

It is important to keep in mind that the word "project" implies that we have a professional management of the integration leveraging professional project managers, experienced with complex projects and equipped with skills of a certified project manager. We should also have a project steering committee in place that has wide competencies and can drive and take decisions quickly.

The word "project" implies that we have a work breakdown structure of the tasks to be executed in the project. Frequent acquirers have a template work breakdown structure that they adapt to each of the new merger integration projects. This ensures completeness and it also allows a proper judgement if we have enough resources assigned and if the resources know what to do in the merger integration.

But we also focus on getting answers to questions like: Do we have the right assignments of resources to merger integration tasks? Are the resources capable of executing their assigned tasks? Do the resources have appropriate social competences to lead people and convince them the integration is the right thing to do?

4.8 Takeaways from chapter 4

It was all about due diligence in this chapter. Starting with definitions, which allow us to phrase our arguments more precisely, we analyzed the purchase decision and different due diligence tasks. This will help us to make sure we understand and execute due diligence tasks properly.

We also listed classical types of due diligence activities and mapped them to the enterprise architecture. From the frequency of due diligence types we learned that it is important to run all types of due diligence if possible to get a full picture of the target and to be able to prepare better for merger integration.

Then we described due diligence as a modeling activity and we analysed numerous inherent challenges, which allows us to cope better with these challenges. At the end of the chapter we focused on merger integration due diligence, defined the task and described the details.

5. Handling risks in merger due diligence

Risks are all around us. So they are also present in mergers and acquisitions. Actually, acquisitions and merger integrations have a bad reputation due to risk. Many integrations fail or do not reach objectives in a sufficient manner. This is why it is important to detect, evaluate and to manage risk in M&A transactions and in merger integration.

Managers should be equipped with the background knowledge about how to handle uncertainty and risks in mergers and acquisitions. For this reason this chapter provides the basics as well as detail information about the sources and types of risks you will meet in merger situations. It also provides an approach how to detect, analyse and treat risk as well as an approach for continuous learning to handle upcoming mergers better.

5.1 Probability, Likelihood and the Black Swan

Managers have two problems: they have to handle complex projects and they have a hard time managing uncertainty. To manage uncertainty, you need knowledge about probability and likelihood.

Probability and likelihood

Probability is a mathematical term. It tells you how probable it is that something is happening. One key prerequisite for using probabilities ist that you know the distribution, meaning that you know about which events tend to happen when and that you know all possible events.

Probability is a great concept, but comes with a pitfall: It can only be used when you know exactly what the distribution is and if you know all the possible events. In mergers and acquisition situations you don't know the distribution. And in many cases you do not know all possible events.

Handling risks in merger due diligence

Example

Let us look at a popular risk of mergers and acquisitions: attrition. Attrition is reduction of workforce by people leaving the company. People in the acquired company have all the knowledge how to build products and how to run the company. So you tend to keep them to ensure continuation of the business. If you acquire a company you simply do not know the acquired people and you do not know if they would like to stay with the new company. How do you tell what the probability is? There is no way to tell.

So what can we do about it? We can use the term likelihood. Whenever you feel, anticipate, guess or derive from experience how likely an event is, you can use likelihood. It is not exact science, so we have to be careful. Likelihood is just a guess.

Example

Let us say we think the likelihood of key people attrition, i.e. key people leaving the company, is 10 percent. Then this ten percent likelihood maybe derived from earlier mergers and acquisitions projects. Great. But be careful here. Since we do not know the exact distribution, we cannot feel safe. This time and in this merger, everything might be different.

But science has some help here. The maximum likelihood method tells us that in case you do not know the likelihood that something happens or not, the best assumption is 50 percent likelihood. Unfortunately this is not providing any help beyond common sense, because something can happen or not, which implies 50 percent likelihood anyway.

So how do we handle uncertainty and likelihoods. My proposal is to start with 50 percent likelihood and then adapt likelihood based on experience and risk mitigations, which we will explain later.

You might say, assuming 50 percent likelihood for each event might be too high. Granted. But assuming a 50 percent likelihood allows you to

Handling risks in merger due diligence

prepare for the worst and also allows you to not be surprised if something adverse happens.

The Black Swan

So we use likelihoods and experience to guess happening of events. So you think you know your risks, you know their likelihoods. Imagine a situation where either a risk with very low likelihood may hit you on day one or a risk hits you that you did not look at. This is what I call a black swan risk.

The term black swan comes from history, where experienced researchers did not believe there would be black swans. Going to Australia they suddenly met black swans! This encounter shocked them, because they were deceived by their long research experience. So be careful with assumptions.

So what is the implication for mergers? Success in merger risk management seems to largely depend on experience. Experience is good, but it does not protect you from the unexpected. My proposal is that you get experience from the book called "Deals from hell" that tells you about many bad experiences in merger situations. So you will be better prepared for your own merger experiences and you know what to avoid and what to monitor as a risk.

5.2   Foundations of risks and risk management

Definition of risk

In this book, we define a risk as an event that has a certain likelihood to occur.

Definition of issue

An issue is a risk that actually has happened or has a likelihood of 100 percent of happening during the acquisition or during the merger integration project. An issue in each acquisition is fear, uncertainty and doubt in employees.

Handling risks in merger due diligence

The big difference between risks and issues is, that you must define and execute mitigations for each issue to avoid adverse effects on merger integration results. There is also a relationship between issues and risks, since many potential risks may turn into issues during due diligence.

You typically start with a large amount of potential risks and try to eliminate potential risk over time or you turn potential risks into issues, which raises the amount of issues over time.

Risks and issues during due diligence

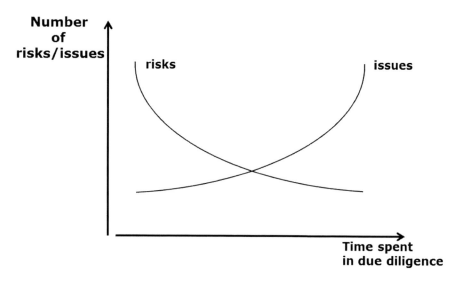

Figure 49: Risks and issues over time in due diligence

Definition of deal breaker

A deal breaker is either

☐ a risk with high likelihood and catastrophic impact on the deal, the integration process, the acquirer, the target or the merged entity; or

Handling risks in merger due diligence

❏ an issue with catastrophic impact on the deal, the integration process, the acquirer, the target or the merged entity.

The name speaks for itself. A deal breaker is something you cannot accept, it will break the deal. In merger due diligence you want to make sure you are able to identify all deal breakers. You can simply classify any risk or issue as a deal breaker, so you can keep track of the deal breakers.

Definition of risk management

Risk management is a task with the goal of detecting, evaluating, treating and monitoring risk.

5.3   Detection of risks in general

You can only handle risks that you know about. So detection of risks is paramount. So let us drill into detection of risks.

How can you detect risks?

Especially important is a structured approach and considering the acquisition and integration from a neutral viewpoint. The structured approach is based on several steps outlined below and a company-specific risk catalog, which is used in every due diligence. A risk workshop together with the Risk Manager will identify and assess the project specific risks.

Also important is the neutral viewpoint. The viewing of the acquisition and integration plans from a neutral position means questioning of hypotheses regarding the acquisition and integration and the "hardening" of the acquisition and integration planning. This viewpoint is usually taken from the finance or central units to support acquisitions in companies.

Common approaches of detecting risks

A common approach is to use a catalog of potential risks and walk through them. This is good if and only if the catalog of risks corresponds well to the case under investigation. So a catalog of risks is only good for generic risks that might occur in every merger. I propose to use a catalog

Handling risks in merger due diligence

of risks as a checklist only in addition to the detection of risks outlined in the next section.

5.4   Detection of risks in merger due diligence

Which merger integration risks are the most common? My experience shows that there are risks that exist in every acquisition and therefore must always be monitored. These risks are departure of employees, cultural integration issues as well as the underestimation of integration effort and of the project management challenges of complex integrations.

The question arises how to build a "complete" model of all risks and to avoid blind spots in the analysis. My proposal is to use the following steps to build a risk model:

❏ risks of the transaction,

❏ risks of the acquiring company,

❏ risks of the target company,

❏ merger integration risk.

Detecting risks for the transaction

We make use of interaction models to detect risks. Using interaction models to determine risks has the advantage that you make a difference between the entities and their relationships. Another advantage is that you include the environment of the acquirer and the target. Defining risk for the transaction is done in two steps: determine risks of the acquirer for the transaction and determine risks of the target regarding the transaction. In addition, please be reminded of the deal dynamics discussion in the foundations of M&A section.

Handling risks in merger due diligence

Example

Risk in acquisition transactions

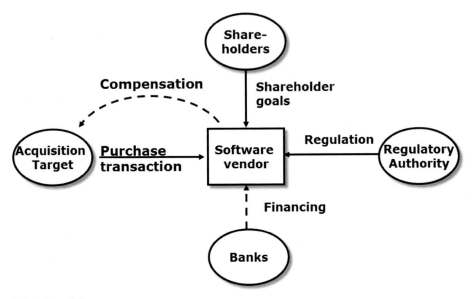

© Dr. Karl Popp 2013

Figure 50: Deriving risks from the transaction interaction diagram

In Figure 50 we show an acquiring software vendor and its transaction relevant environment like e.g. Akquisition target, Shareholders, Regulatory Authorities and *Banks.*

For each object and relationship we define risks and issues and put them on a list. For each object, you can look at risks of the status of the object, how the object might influence the process of the merger transaction and how the behavior of an object might change and impact the merger transaction.

Handling risks in merger due diligence

Example

Looking at Figure 50, we can look at Regulatory Authorities and their impact on the acquirer based on the Regulation relationship. A risk might be that the authorities might not approve the deal and pending approvals might delay the deal timeframes.

If you look at the shareholders of the acquirer, they might be involved in the decision process and their behavior and their expectations for a merger transaction might be important for the merger transaction. One risk might be that if the shareholders have to approve the deal, they might take an adverse decision.

To determine risks of the target regarding the transaction we repeat the same step with the target in focus. We look at the interaction diagram of the target in context with the acquisition and carry out the steps mentioned above.

Defining risks for the target company

For target company risks, we look at the interaction diagram of the normal business of the target and define risks and issues for each object and each relationship.

For due diligence, this means that each instance of a supplier and each instance of a customer relationship can carry risks. There is also risk in the contracts, products delivered and payments to be done that are existent in each instance of supplier and customer relationships. Let us start with a simple example.

Handling risks in merger due diligence

Interaction model of the Business Strategy and business plan layer

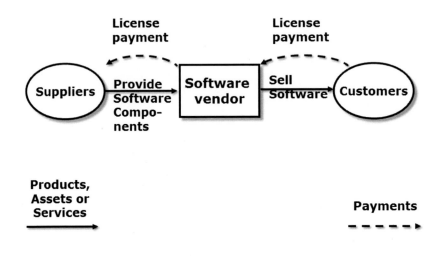

© Dr. Karl Popp 2012

Figure 51: Deriving risks from the target interaction diagram

Example

Based on the simplified interaction model in Figure 51 we can define risks. Starting from the left, we define risks for Suppliers. We look at suppliers in general, identify e.g. key suppliers, to which a critical dependency exists and list corresponding risks. Looking at a relationship, e.g. Sell software between the software vendor and the Customers object, we can look at risks in this relationship, e.g. commitments to customers which might impose a risk on post merger integration plans. If significant parts of the future development capacity of the software vendors were committed to customers, this might limit the capacity for merger integration work and e.g. for integration of products of the acquirer and the target's products.

Handling risks in merger due diligence

While this simple example already generates several risks, let us have a look at a more realistic example and derive some risks there.

Example

Software vendor interaction model and risk

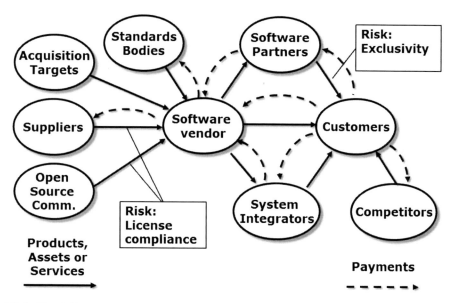

© Dr. Karl Popp 2013

Figure 52: Deriving risks from the interaction diagram

To define risks in this model means to define risks for each of the 9 entities and each of the 18 relationships. Let us focus on some popular risks here.

The object Software Partners delivers software to customers. Let us assume this is a resell relationship. One risk might be that there are exclusive resell rights in one of the instances of this relationship. We might not want to acquire a company where a partner has exclusive resell rights, so the target would have to change that contract with the partner accordingly.

We make use of open source software provided by the object Open Source Community. A typical risk is that we are not in compliance with the open source license terms. So as a mitigation we would have to have a complete list of open source software used in the target products and check compliance with the corresponding license terms.

The target also makes use of Suppliers' software as part of the target solutions. A risk is that the target might not have appropriate third party rights for all delivery models and business models for the software. For mitigation of that risk we would have to check all of the target's supplier relationships and contracts to make sure the target is in compliance with the supplier license terms and has appropriate rights for all delivery models like Software as a service or on demand.

Risks of the merger integration

To determine risks of the merger integration we have to recap what merger integration means. As you can see in Figure 53 the merger integration risk is the combination of risk of the integration project and the risk in the merged organization.

While the risk in the merged organization can be evaluated as explained above, the risk of the merger integration needs to be elaborated. We see the following categories of risks in merger integration:

❑ Risk in the merger integration task, which means we are not reaching goals and objectives of the merger integration task as planned;

❑ Risk in the merger integration project

  o Project organization and resources

  o Project processes (merger integration process),

  o Complexity of the merger integration

Handling risks in merger due diligence

Risk of merger integration

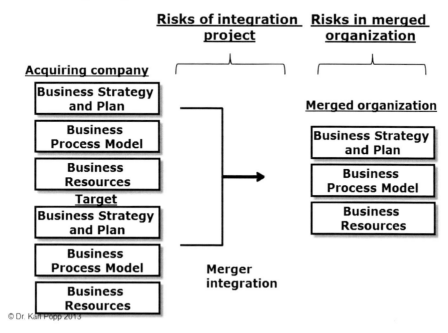

Figure 53: Risks of merger integration

Risk in the merger integration task

Looking at the task we can derive the risk lying in it. The highest impact risk of a task is if the goal cannot be reached. We would consider the merger integration a failure if the acquired entity would not be integrated into the new entity. So each merger integration has one dealbreaker risk: Goal of merger integration not reached.

If the goal can be reached, there still might be trouble if one or several of the objectives of the merger integration cannot be reached. I recommend to create a risk for each of the objectives of the merger integration to make sure the risks are monitored and properly mitigated.

Merger integration task

© Dr. Karl Popp 2013

Figure 54: Risk in merger integration task

Since we also know the composition of the task *Merger Integration*, we should also look at potential risk of the decomposed tasks. Potential risks exist in the design of the new entity, in planning merger integration and in the execution of the merger integration project, which we will look at in detail now.

Handling risks in merger due diligence

Decomposing the merger integration task

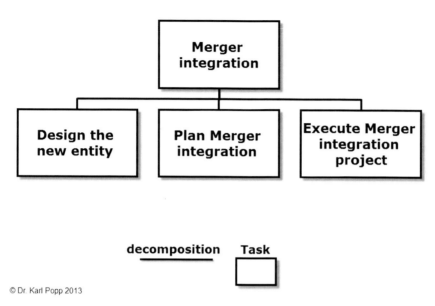

© Dr. Karl Popp 2013

Figure 55: Risk in decomposed merger integration task

Risks in the merger integration project

As mentioned above the first category of risks in the merger integration project are lying within the project organization and project resources. Sufficient knowledgable people have to be assigned for project management and execution, from the target and from the acquirer. These resources should be able to dedicate enough time to execution of merger integration tasks. From a practitioners view, the last two sentences contain at least six potential risks, since you often do not get sufficient resources, which might not be knowledgable with regard to merger integration or they might not get assigned at all to the merger integration project. Review all aspects and add risks to the list.

Handling risks in merger due diligence

The second category of risks reside within project processes (merger integration processes). The process might be non-existent or badly defined or designed, which poses a huge risk for successfully executing merger integrations. Even in experienced, frequent acquirers some missing processes have to be created on the fly during the merger integration project. Make sure you have these risks on your radar.

As mentioned in earlier chapters, merger integration projects have a specific complexity. Make sure you determine the complexity of your merger integration project and add risks if needed. Popular risks are: complexity is much higher than expected, resulting in late delivery of work packages. The number of assigned resources might be too small for the integration work, which is an additional risk of delays and low quality execution of the merger integration project.

5.5   Evaluation of risks

We compare risk based on their expected value. Expected value is value of the damage multiplied with the likelihood of the risk.

Based on the experience with black swan risks it also makes sense to look at high damage risks without looking at the probability. Figure out how you would deal with such a risk in advance or develop countermeasures to avoid the risks.

Steps in evaluating risks

The steps in evaluation of risks are:

❐   List all risks based on the approach listed above.

❐   Determine the worst case impact of each risk.

❐   Determine the likelihood based on the hints explained earlier.

❐   Multiply impact with likelihood and compare the risks.

Example

Evaluation of risks

Risk	Impact	Likeli-hood	Expected value in USD
Exclusive resell for the US	Revenue loss of -1.000.000 USD	50%	-500.000
Non-compliance with open source licenses	Product has to be open sourced, no revenue possible -5.000.000 USD	50%	-2.500.000
Too much capacity of the target dedicated to customers in the future	Delay of revenue -250.000 USD	50%	-125.000

© Dr. Karl Popp 2013

Figure 56: Evaluation of risks

We have collected the risks of the last examples in this section into a list of risks, we have estimated the negative impact and documented it in column Impact. Then we added likelihoods and calculated the expected value.

As we can see, open source license compliance has the largest negative expected value in our example. This risk is the first one to mitigate or to eliminate.

Handling risks in merger due diligence

5.6 Treatment of risks

Based on the identified and evaluated risk we now define the treatment of these risks. Here are the options:

☐ Ignore,

☐ Mitigate,

☐ Escalate.

Ignoring risk

Ignoring risk is a good strategy for risks that have a very very low likelihood and very low impact on the merger integration. For all other risk ignoring is not a good strategy.

Mitigate

For most of the risks (and all issues) you will end up defining mitigation tasks and executing these tasks during the merger integration project. In addition you need to monitor the risk frequently during merger integration.

Escalate

Escalation to management is the perfect way to treat deal breakers. Report the risk to management with proposed mitigations and a clearly defined decision proposal.

Sell risk

Some large impact risks cannot be properly mitigated. In this case you might consider selling the risk to an insurance company.

Example

If you bought a software company in India including their buildings and you run a risk that the the soil might be contaminated, you can try to sell this risk to an insurance company.

5.7 Experience management for risk management

Here is my eternal wisdom from best practices that I use, based on risks and risk management, in each project:

Leave room for uncertainty

Even if you diligently worked on risk analysis and risk management, there still is uncertainty in all aspects of mergers and acquisitions. Likelihoods might not be correct, risks and impacts you have not foreseen might hit you. Get prepared for dealing with it by giving risks and planning some room regarding timing of activities, budget etc.

Establish direct executive involvement and attention

For risk management, you need frequent executive attention and involvement. Executives are a great help for preventing and treating risks but also for post mortem treatment of unexpected risks that have happened.

Establish ways to often and quickly take decisions

How would you prepare to have your executives take 1.000 urgent decisions for your project in two months? Think about it. Many risks in mergers and acquisition projects come from late or delayed decisions. The answer is simple: have frequent executive meetings where decisions are taken.

Handling risks in merger due diligence

Leverage experience management for your purposes

With every acquisition as a frequent acquirer, you can improve the risk catalog and the likelihoods of risks. You will also get better in determining sizes of buffers in project and budget planning for the post merger integration.

Update and enrich the risk catalog after each acquisition

Add new risks that you have met and also add mitigations that were typically used. Tweak existing risk definitions and ratings to optimize the risk catalog.

5.8   Takeaways from chapter 5

After looking at some theoretical background of risks and some definitions, we used the risk management definition to define activities important for risk management in due diligence: detection of risks, evaluation of risks as well as treatment and monitoring of risk. At the end of the chapter, impact, handling and management of risks in real life projects were summarized in a section about continuous learning for risk management.

6. Foundations of the software business and their relevance for due diligence

Mergers and acquisitions in the software business have specifics of that industry that require basic understanding of underlying patterns and concepts of the software business. In this chapter we will explain the software business. In addition, we will always mark acquisition and merger integration relevant aspects in a box like the one around this paragraph.

Let us take two views of a software company, an outside view (layer 1) and an inside view (layer 2). The outside view contains the business strategy and business plan and shows all relationships with the outside world that relate to products and services provided from or to the software vendor. In the software industry, there are numerous typical product and service relationships that make the software industry special and also allow a standardization of the due diligence of these types of relationships. Business models are part of the business plan and belong to layer 1. This chapter is based on the book "Profit from software ecosystems" (Meyer, 2011).

6.1   A general classification of business models

A business model tells you what the business of a company is all about. It tells you which goods or services are provided by a company and how the company is compensated for the goods and services. Since our focus is the software industry, all businesses provide goods and services around software. In this chapter, we will learn about different business models and we will find out that not all businesses in the software industry are the same. This chapter will also give you the tools to design a business model for your company in the software industry.

By extending the classification of business models from MIT Sloan School of Management [Wei+05], we will look at different business models in the software industry. Using this model, you will be able to classify the business model of a software vendor. Later we will show how the different business models are implemented by software vendors.

A **business model** tells which goods or services are provided by a company and how the company is compensated for the goods and services. Formally, the business model consists of three things: the type of goods/services provided, the Business Model Archetype and a revenue model. A business model is a model on type level, which means that it is a generic model showing the type of business, but not how the business is run.

Business Model

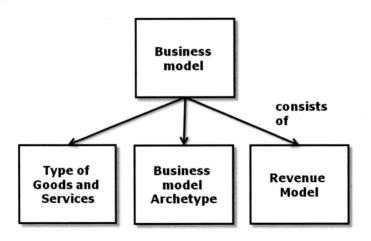

Figure 57: Business models

As we will see later in this book, a company can choose more than one combination of goods and services, archetype and revenue model. This combination can be a source of competitive advantage, esp. when one business model feeds another business model at the same company. One

Page 126

example is Google's search and advertising business, which provides funding for the numerous other businesses Google is running.

We use business models as an anchor point for further analysis of the target and of merger integration. We will analyse typical synergies, risks, integration aspects with specific business models to ensure we do not forget these attributes when we meet certain business models.

Business Model and Operations Model

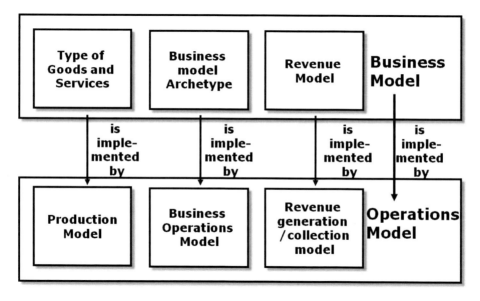

Copyright © 2009 Synomic GmbH

Figure 58: Business model and operations model

A business model can be implemented in an **operations model**. The operations model shows how the business is run and how the resources of the business run the corresponding business processes in the company. Looking at the three components of the business model each of them gets implemented as part of the Operations model.

Foundations of the software business and their relevance for due diligence

The type of goods/services gets implemented in the Production Model. It defines which processes and organizations create the goods/services. For a software vendor, software usually gets created by the development organization by executing development processes.

The business model archetype gets implemented in the business operations model. In the software industry, for the IP lessor business of licensing software to customers, appropriate processes and organizations will market and sell the software vendor´s solutions to customers.

The revenue model gets implemented in the Revenue generation/collection model. In this chapter we focus on the business model and its components and the choices a software vendor has for each of the three components of the business model.

> Regarding due diligence there are several items to be analysed. The production model, business operations model and revenue generation model used have to be identified and understood. There are, of course, several dimensions to this, which are covered in due diligence activities like market, commercial, tax and human resources due diligence. During this analysis, risks will be identified and listed accordingly.

Types of goods

We make use of the Type of Goods and Business Model Archetype defined by Weill et al (Weill 2005).

Goods are products and services offered. The types of goods are:

- **financial goods** (cash and other assets),
- **physical goods** (real, physical products, durable and non-durable goods),
- **intangible goods** (software but also other intellectual property, knowledge and brand image) and
- **human goods** (people´s time and effort).

Types of goods and services

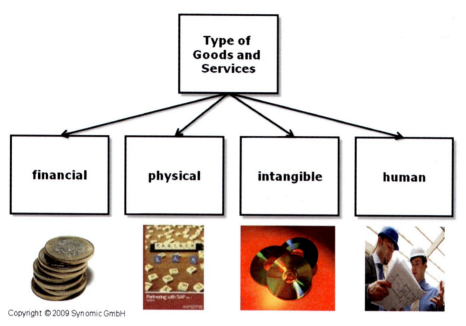

Figure 59: Types of goods and services

Looking at types of goods, we find matching due diligence activites as outlined later in this book, like IP due diligence for intangible goods, HR due diligence for human goods etc.

Business Model Archetypes

Business Model Archetypes are basic patterns of doing business. Available archetypes are creator, distributor, lessor and broker.

A **creator** uses supplied goods and internal assets and transforms them to create a product sold to customers. It is important to know that the main work done by the creator is designing the product. An example is Apple. Apple designs the iPod in California. So Apple is a creator.

Foundations of the software business and their relevance for due diligence

A **distributor** buys a product and provides the same product to customers. Obvious examples are companies in the wholesale and retail industries, like Sears or Saks, or Apple's retail store for applications, the iTunes AppStore.

A **lessor** provides the temporary right to use, but not own, a product or service to customers. Examples are landlords, lenders of money, consultants and software companies that license their software to customers. For human services, HR brokers lend their employees' time to customers.

	Type of Products/Services offered			
	Financial	Physical	Intangible	Human
Creator	Entrepreneur	Manufacturer	Inventor	n/a
Distributor	Financial trader	Wholesaler, Retailer	IP distributor	n/a
Lessor	Financial lessor	Physical lessor	IP lessor	Contractor
Broker	Financial broker	Physical broker	IP broker	HR broker

Figure 60: Business model archetypes and types of goods. Source: [Wei+05, 31], amended by author

A **broker** facilitates the matching of potential buyers and sellers. A broker never takes ownership of the products and services. An example is a stock broker. Another example is Google's advertising business, which matches the advertiser with potential customers.

Figure 60 shows the combination of archetypes and type of goods offered, resulting in 16 different business model types.

Each of the business model archetypes has generic chances, risks, critical success factors, cost structure and pricing models as well as typical topics to investigate. In software companies, we often find several business model archetypes implemented that create a hybrid business model. In this case, the combination of business model archetypes makes up the business model of the company.

Disruptive business models

Disruptive business models are business models that change the rules of the game, e.g. by offering of products free of charge in a market that did not have free of charge offerings. These disruptive business models are very often hybrid models, which means that the business of providing the free-of-charge product is often funded by one or many other businesses. Popular examples are Google´s business model, where ads pay for several free of charge business models and Microsoft´s business model for internet browsers, where other revenues pay for the development and maintenance of the browser or Salesforce´s cloud only business model.

For due diligence, disruptive business models are a challenge due to their exceptional character. They do not allow for reusing existing results or learnings from other due diligences.

6.2   Specifics of Inventors

Inventors create intangible goods like services or intangible products. The main task is inventing (designing) the new service or product. Often this is an expensive task, esp. when the inventor designs and programs software leveraging developers on his own payroll.

Cost

There is the common assumption that there are significant sunk cost (for development) before a software solution can be sold and compensated for. This is only the case, if there is cost of development and the customers do not provide funding before the software is shipped. If the software is built

Page 131

specifically for one customer, there usually is funding by the customer to have the software built to order.

In general, it makes sense for inventors to get at least partial funding from customers and to try to lower the cost of development. Funding can come from the maintenance revenue that is provided by existing customers.

Cost savings can be achieved by trying to automate development or by reducing sourcing cost. Sourcing cost can be reduced by hiring developers in low cost countries or by making massive use of free of charge open source software or by leveraging the open source community to build the software.

Another option is to license third party software instead of having employees coding the solutions.

After invention, software products are being licensed, rented or provided as a service to customers by IP Lessors.

> In due diligence, we must review the creation and protection of intellectual property carefully for an Inventor business model. We also check the ways how the inventors license the intellectual property to customers and how they use third party intellectual property to create their products in one of the following chapters.

6.3   Specifics of IP Lessors

IP Lessors are providing intangible goods "for rent" to customers. As outlined above, intangible goods can be software but also other intellectual property, like knowledge, brand image, trade secrets or patents.

Delivery models and cost

Software can be provided to the customer as a product or as a service. It can be provided by the software vendor or by a partner.

Delivery models and business models

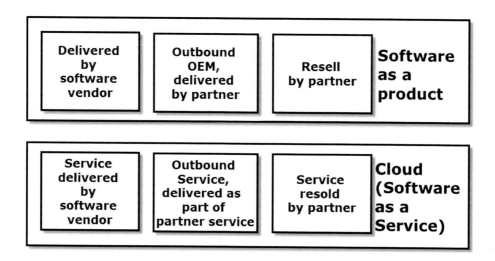

© Dr. Karl Popp 2012

Figure 61: Delivery models and business models

Provisioning a product means that the software product gets shipped to the customer and the customer gets usage rights for a specified purpose. This covers on premise and on device models, e.g. the software can run on a computer or a mobile device.

The customer does not get ownership of a product, but rights to use the software for a specified compensation. Usually that compensation is a fee. Cost of support and of providing maintenance releases is carried by the IP Lessor or by the partner. The cost of operations of the solution is carried by the customer.

Provisioning a service means that the customer gets access to the software as well as usage rights for a specified time and a specified purpose. The software runs at a hosting provider or in the cloud. The IP Lessor or

Foundations of the software business and their relevance for due diligence

the partner carries the cost of providing support and providing maintenance releases as well as the cost of operations of the solution. The customer carries the cost for the service.

Looking at the software industry, most software companies have a hybrid business model, because they are acting as an inventor and as an IP Lessor at the same time. We also see that an increasing number of software companies deliver their software both as a product and as a service either directly or through partner channels to customers.

> Important for due diligence is that we list all delivery models, analyze them separately, decide if we would like to keep them in the merged entity and plan supporting merger integration activities accordingly. It is important to note that cloud delivery models differ substantially from software as a product. From a viewpoint of using third party software for cloud services, the rights needed for offering a service are different from rights needed to ship a product, not to mention that delivery and support services are also different.

6.4   Revenue models

A **revenue model** defines how a company is compensated for the goods and services provided. The compensation usually, but not necessarily, is a payment. An entrepreneur has the freedom to create a revenue model for his company´s products and services. We will show that a company can choose from a variety of revenue models for its goods and services.

Example

One simple example is a barber who gets compensated for each of his services (haircut, shave) each time they are consumed. He gets compensated by the customer in the form of credit card or cash payments.

A revenue model consists of one or several **revenue streams** [see Oster04]. Usually a revenue stream compensates for each one of the goods and services offered. But this is not necessarily the case. A company can choose to offer three services and only get paid for one of the services. We will see more examples later in this chapter.

Example

To use the simple barber example, the barber offers haircut and shave as a Contractor and acts as a retailer for hair care products. He receives revenue streams from haircut service, from shaving service and from hair care products he is selling to customers.

Revenue Model and Revenue Streams Example

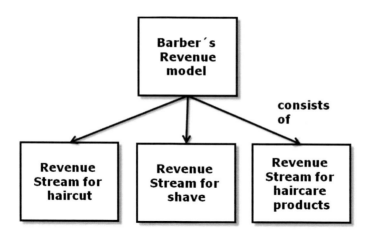

Figure 62: Revenue model and revenue streams example

Important for due diligence is that we list all revenue streams, analyze them and decide if we would like to keep them and plan corresponding merger integration activities. One key activity is to check the effect of

Foundations of the software business and their relevance for due diligence

applying the revenue recognition guidelines from the acquiring company to the target.

There are flexible ways to create revenue streams for the goods and services provided. Different types of revenue streams are created by choosing different values for the following **attributes of a revenue stream**:

☐ **Compensator**: Party, which provides the compensation (customer or third parties).

☐ **Effect**: it tells what the effect of the compensation is (no compensation, compensation in goods or services, compensation by different forms of payment).

☐ **Causality** Link: Reference from the compensation to the goods and services (per good/service, per bundle of goods and services compensated for).

☐ **Rating and Charging model**: this model tells for each compensation, how the usage or consumption is rated and how it is charged for.

☐ **Pricing**: there are different pricing mechanisms and strategies available, which we relate to below.

☐ **Timing**: tells at what time the compensation will happen (prepay, by payment schedule, post consumption).

Compensator, Effect and Causality

In this chapter we will look at if and why there is compensation, and who provides the compensation.

Compensator

In the creation of a revenue model, you first look at the different parties which could provide the compensation. A simple case of a compensator for goods and services is that a customer pays in cash for each instance of a service that was consumed. This again relates to our simple barber example, in which the barber charges the customers for shaving.

But compensation can be more complex in real life. Sometimes the customer does not pay at all for the services provided, but a third party. An example is Google's search service, which is free of charge for customers, but is paid for by third parties, in this case the advertisers.

Effect

What is the effect of the compensation? It tells if compensation takes place and of what type the compensation is:

❏ A good or a service might have **no compensation**. An example is open source software, which can be used without monetary compensation under a certain license. Another example is the social work of a volunteer.

❏ A good or a service might be compensated with **other goods and services** in return. The search service from Google is compensated with information about the searching user.

❏ A good or a service might be compensated financially by **different forms of payment**. An obvious example is the barber, who gets compensated by cash or credit card payments.

Causality

A compensation or revenue stream can be linked to one or more goods and services provided (**Causality**). A good example is software as a service. The service "Software as a service" consists of the four services provide software, operate (run) the software, maintain the software and support the software. The customer compensates for the bundle of these four services with one payment per month, per number of users.

A revenue stream can also link to one or more instances of the same good or service provided. If a customer pays for software usage by one hundred employees, then this payment relates to one hundred instances of the service "Usage of software by one user".

Foundations of the software business and their relevance for due diligence

Example

An example is a commercial open source company company. It provides open source software to customers for free. The company also offers chargeable support services and maintenance services to customers, which are compensated by one joint revenue stream for support and maintenance. Since there is no compensation for usage of the software, the revenue stream for support and maintenance has to be big enough to cover the cost of creation, support and maintenance of the open source software.

Rating and Charging

In this chapter we are looking at how consumptions of goods and services are rated and charged for.

Rating

Rating is defined as the **way to measure** the usage or consumption of goods and services. Ratings are done based on amounts or on time or ratings are combinations of both.

Ratings by amount are based on the number of goods and services consumed. There are many different ratings possible and many different ratings are used in practice.

Typical ratings by amount in the software industry are the number of processors of a computer that runs software or the number of users that has access to a software solution or the throughput of a software solution. A software as a service provider usually rates the number of users that have access to the offering.

Ratings by time are also popular. You could allow the usage of a software or service for a limited time or for a certain period of time. A cell phone network provider could for example rate for initiation of a call and for each minute of the call by one minute increments.

Foundations of the software business and their relevance for due diligence

Rating

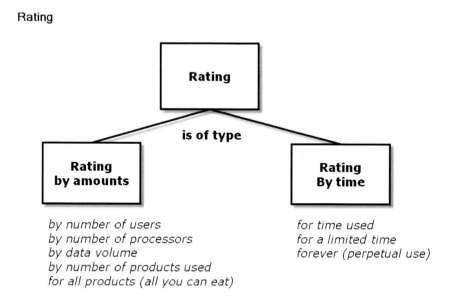

Figure 63: Types of Ratings

Charging

Charging is defined as the **way to define the compensation amount for a certain rating** of goods and service consumption. There is again tremendous freedom to create charging rules. Typical charging models in the software industry are fixed fees for each processor of a server or fixed fees per user or fixed fee per megabyte throughput for a data cleansing solution or a combination of the above.

Foundations of the software business and their relevance for due diligence

Example

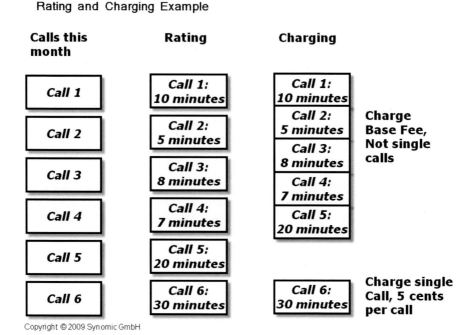

Figure 64: Rating and charging example

Using the cell phone example, the cell phone network provider would use ratings by time. He could charge five cent per minute for the call. In addition, charging could also define that the cell phone network provider does not charge for the first five calls in a month, because they are bundled and included in the base fee. All following calls that month are charged with five cents. Rating and charging for this case is depicted in Figure 64. The base fee could be five dollars. Only call six is rated by time and charged for with five cents per minute (30 minutes multiplied with 5 cents per minute).

It is also possible to charge a minimum amount every month for using the cell phone network, which is independent of the number of calls. As you

Foundations of the software business and their relevance for due diligence

can see, this leads to a large number of possible charging models for the usage of cell phone networks.

Extreme examples of rating and charging in the software industry are perpetual licenses and all you can eat licenses. **Perpetual license** means that a revenue stream relates to perpetual use of a software component, which means that the software can be used forever. So the usage is rated by time for unlimited time, but compensated for perpetual use.

An **all you can eat license** might refer to the customer having a right to use all software solutions of a software vendor. In this case, the software vendor is bundling all of its products into one bundle. This is usually done for large customers. It is a good way to sell more products into a customer and to lock-out competitors from that customer.

> In due diligence we will check if the rating and charging fits the strategy of the acquiring entity and if the acquiring entity is capable of executing the rating and charging within its administration. If products of the acquired entity are to be continued to be sold, pricing must be streamlined, too.

Pricing

As soon as a good or service consumption has been rated and charging is defined, we are ready to look at the price for a certain rating and charging. We will look at three mechanisms to determine the price: vendor set pricing, customer set pricing and market pricing.

Vendor set pricing

It is important to emphasize, that the software vendor defines a **proposed price**. If the customers are willing to pay this price is not guaranteed. This depends on the market for the software products under consideration, esp. the competition of software vendors in this market.

In addition, customers know that a software vendor has very low marginal cost for an additional copy of the software. If the customer position is strong enough, he might want to negotiate for **discounts**. In some cases

Foundations of the software business and their relevance for due diligence

the price is not negotiable, esp. when there is a strong position of the software vendor or a weak position of companies using the software.

Software vendors often give **discounts on a first sale** to a customer to create lock-in for the customer by having the customer use the software vendor´s products. If the customer uses the products and the cost to switch to another product are significant, a **customer lock-in** is created. For the software vendor, this is insurance for future maintenance and support revenue (and cost).

Another opportunity for the vendor in customer lock-in is an **up sell opportunity**. This is based on the software vendor´s expectation, that there is an opportunity to sell additional, complementing products or additional licenses for products to that customer later on.

There are numerous pricing mechanisms and strategies. Since we do not focus on pricing in this book, we will have a look at different pricing models along Figure 65 for an overview. For details on pricing mechanisms see [Oste04]. For details of pricing strategies for software vendors see [Bux+08].

Let us start with a simple example. A software vendor wants to charge for the usage of a complete product, which means that the software vendor sets a fixed price for the rated use of the product as a whole. This leads to three **fixed price models** which are popular in the software industry: pay per use, subscription and list price.

A **pay per use** model, is defined in a way that a customer is rated for actual use and charged for the amount of actual use. The software vendor sets a fixed price. This relates to line 1 in Figure 65.

A **subscription pricing model** defines that consumption is rated by the period of time available to the customer for consumption, not by actual use. The customer has to pay the price even if there is no consumption of products and services. Example is access to an online marketplace for one month for a fixed price or a subscription to a data feed for one month.

A **list price** is usually rated by the amount of planned use and charged for per product and planned use. A list price means that a vendor sets the price and a customer can get the products for that price listed in the price list.

In addition to these fixed price models, we have listed three models, where the price per product/service is variable, which is called **differential pricing**.

A simple example is **feature dependent pricing** meaning that the customer is rated for the product features he is using and charged for by the number of users, time and features used.

Pricing examples

Product Pricing	Pricing model	Rating	Charging	Price is set by
Fixed Pricing per used product	Pay per use	By amount of actual use	per product, user and time	Software vendor
	Subscription	By amount and time for use	per product, user and time	Software vendor
	List price	By amount of planned use	per product, user and time	Software vendor
Differential Pricing for products	Feature dependent	By amount of features	Per feature, user and time	Software vendor
	Volume dependent	By amount of volume	By volume and time	Software vendor
	Value based	By amount of value	By share of customer value	Customer

Figure 65: Typical Pricing examples. Source:[Oste04, 100], adapted by author.

The second example for differential pricing is **volume dependent** meaning that the consumption is rated based on a measure of volume. One

Page 143

example could be an IP-based software PBX system rated by the data volume processed per month. Another example is the use of a SOA messaging platform rated by the number of SOA calls processed per month.

Customer set pricing

When does the customer determine the pricing? There are basically two situations: either the customer has a very strong position in the negotiation with the software vendor or the product or service is priced by the customer value of the product/service.

Relating to Figure 65, this is the third and most appealing differential pricing example called **value based pricing**. The idea is that the customer pays a share of the value that the product or service has created for the customer. Examples are a supply chain solution, which is rated by the cost saved per month, a purchasing service, which is rated by purchasing cost saved by article per year or an inventory management solution rated by keeping appropriate inventory levels at all times.

For a software vendor, this is a very enticing opportunity to maximize profits. Why? Let us assume the share of the customer value is always above a fixed price. When the vendor sells for the fixed price, this price is also the cap on the software vendor´s revenue. When a software vendor can get a share of the customer value, there is no cap on the revenue.

Let us assume, it is unclear, if the share of customer value is above a fixed price. Then the fixed price is more favorable, because the fixed price is a price floor. The price cannot drop below the fixed price, even if the customer value is below expectations.

Since there are no commonly accepted value measures in the industry that are used for value based pricing of software solutions, this is a space, where a lot of innovation will happen.

Discounts

As soon as rating, charging, pricing are defined, you also need a discounting strategy that in return also affects pricing. In a global software

Foundations of the software business and their relevance for due diligence

industry it is important to remark that discounts vary drastically between countries, sectors and customer sizes.

> In due diligence, we have to compare the discount strategy of the acquirer and the target to come to realistic revenue assumptions and to determine changes to be compliant with revenue recognition rules.

Timing of compensation

The **timing** of compensation tells **at what time the compensation will happen and what additional conditions apply** for the timing of the compensation. Simple examples we meet often are

- ❑ **prepay**, which means you pay before you are able to consume goods or services,

- ❑ by **payment schedule**, which might define certain payments at different points in time under certain payment conditions,

- ❑ **post pay**, meaning you pay after you were able to consume or have received or consumed the products or services.

> In due diligence, we have to check if the available target compensation timings are accepted and implementable by the acquirer.

A more complex example is a milestone based payment schedule for a consulting project that shapes the payments as follows: payments are done for 20 percent increments of project completion. This means that project completion is rated by 20 percent increments and charged for by effort spent on the project. That would result in a payment each time the project completion rate has increased by 20 percent.

In the cell phone example the monthly invoice would be 6.50 USD based on the rating explained above. The amount is the sum of the base fee (5 USD) and call six (30 minutes multiplied with 5 cents per minute).

Example

In our barber example, the barber offers two services (haircut and shave) and gets a revenue stream for each of the services offered. He rates per completed service delivery, which means completed haircut or completed shave. He charges a fixed price for each. Timing is immediate. Effect is payment in cash or by credit card.

Revenue Stream Attributes Example

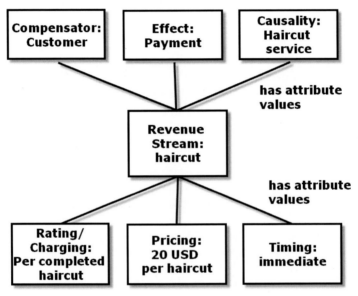

Copyright © 2009 Synomic GmbH

Figure 66: Revenue stream example

The barber could decide to change the causality link by offering haircut and shave for one price. This way he gets one revenue stream for a combination of haircut and shave services. Another way of changing the causality link is to bundle several instances of the same service. The barber could offer ten haircuts for the price of nine haircuts with prepay meaning you pay for ten haircuts in advance.

Foundations of the software business and their relevance for due diligence

> In merger due diligence, list all business models, products, services, bundles and revenue streams. Decide if you would like to change, continue or discontinue these. Decide also how the products and services shall integrate and/or be bundled with the acquirer's products and services. All decisions create workload for the merger integration and should be documented well.

6.5 Intellectual property due diligence

In a knowledge-heavy industry, the utilization of intellectual property is often the core business. The monetization of that intellectual property must be preceded by the creation and protection of intellectual property (IP). IP strategies in the software industry are manifold and often include open and/or closed innovation strategies.

In the software industry intellectual property is often the most important asset of a company. Besides employees and intellectual property there often are no other significant assets or means of production. So to safeguard the existing business of the target, future business and to safeguard that the target really owns their software products, you must carry out IP due diligence.

Foundations of the software business and their relevance for due diligence

Why and how look at IP?

- Why intellectual property due diligence
  - safeguards what you acquire
  - Safeguards the exploitation of what you acquire
- How ?
  - Locates and assesses all Intellectual property
  - Assesses IP „handling" at target
  - Defines the needed IPR for planned utilization

© Dr. Karl Popp 2012

Figure 67: Reasons to look at IP

Next let us look at how is intellectual property generated and leveraged in the software industry?

Usage of intellectual property rights in the software industry

As a prerequisite to leveraging IP for a company, IP to be owned by the company can be created or IP owned by other companies can be used or acquired. In software companies, products are created by own staff (employees) and contracted service providers (suppliers of services). Together with IP owned by other companies, like OEM software, freeware and open source software, this usually leads to a mix of components in a software product (Figure 68).

Types of components of a software product

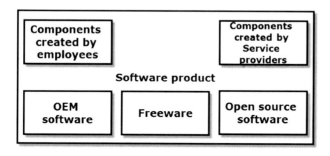

Figure 68: Types of components of a software product

A software vendor can also add new intellectual property to its portfolio by acquiring other companies (acquisition targets). In addition, the software vendor can apply for patents with patent authorities that might grant the patent to the software vendor (Figure 69).

Looking at intellectual property owned by other companies that the software vendor might use, four types are dominant in the software industry: patents, freeware, open source software and third party software.

Foundations of the software business and their relevance for due diligence

Sources of intellectual property

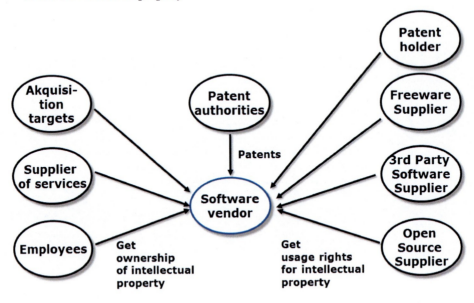

© Dr. Karl Popp 2012

Figure 69: Sources of Intellectual Property

When creating software for customers, software vendors often use (Figure 68):

❏   Software components created by the software vendor´s employees or by service providers,

❏   but also third party software components (OEM software, open source software, freeware).

This usage is based on ownership and usage rights for these components, (see the right hand part of Figure 69). In addition, the software vendor might make use of patents held by other companies by getting a patent license.

From a utilization point of view, software is often licensed by a software vendor to customers for a license fee. In order to assure that the software

Foundations of the software business and their relevance for due diligence

vendor can run the business of licensing the software to customers, the ownership of intellectual property and the usage rights for intellectual property have to be checked. Our special interest here will be on usage rights for third party software, open source software and freeware.

Definition of IP due diligence

A simple definition of IP Due Diligence

- ## Typical definition:
  - Audit of Patents, Know-how, Copyrights, Trade marks, Infringements, Licenses and collaboration agreements
- ## Added here:
  - Scope: employee agreements, Process audit of IP compliance processes
  - Detail: Licenses for patents, third party products, freeware, open source

© Dr. Karl Popp 2012

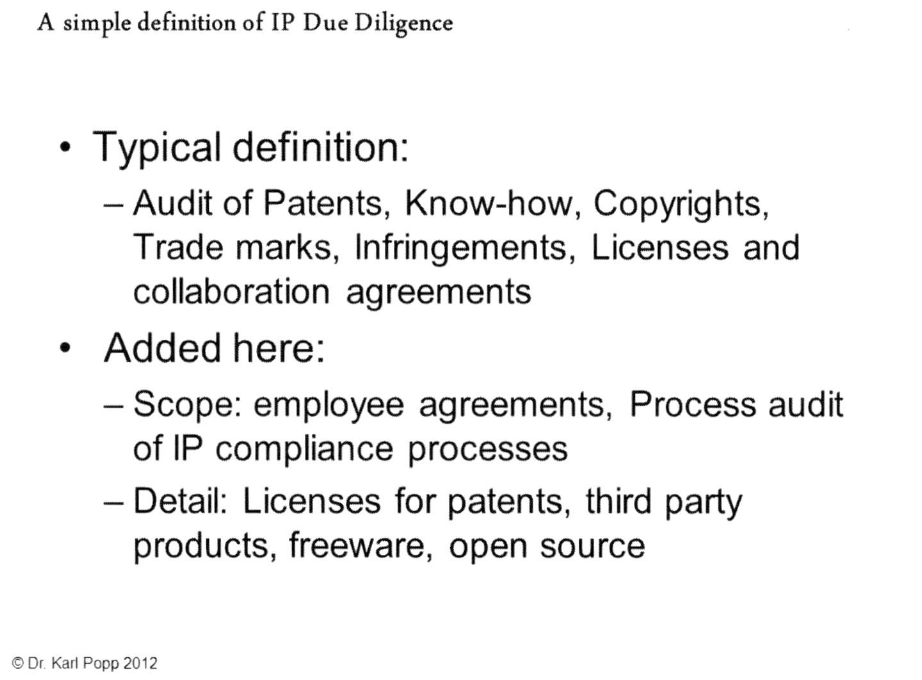

Figure 70: Definition of IP due diligence

So the takeover of such a company is driven by due diligence of intellectual property. You have to dedicate special attention and care to this topic.

So what is important regarding intellectual property if you acquire a software company? In a holistic IP due diligence, the portfolio of intellectual property rights, the software vendor´s relations with all sources of IP and the different types of intended utilization of intellectual property are examined.

Page 151

Check status quo of target IP

- ## Check all sources
  - That intellectual property really belongs to the target
  - That sufficient usage rights are granted to the target
- ## Check all existing utilizations
  - That each utilization is possible based on
    - own intellectual property
    - Usage rights for third party, open source and freeware

© Dr. Karl Popp 2012

Figure 71: How to check the status quo of IP

With the acquisition of a software company the following views on intellectual property are relevant:

❑ The current state and future intentions for utilization of IP;

❑ Status and review of intellectual property rights and intellectual property usage rights at the target.

These considerations bring us to the definition if IP Due Diligence:

IP Due Diligence: For all existing and future utilizations of all target products and services:

❑ determine all intellectual property rights and obligations, subsidiary measures, related fees and payments, compliance processes, potential and existing litigations and infringements related to the target and its products and services; and

☐ examine and evaluate these to ensure that the target has ownership of the IP to be sold and that the existing and future utilizations are in compliance with the IP rights owned by the target.

Let us start with the utilization first, because the utilization of IP will give us requirements for the review of IP rights and IP usage rights.

Review of the utilization of intellectual property

Utilization means the ways in which a software vendors wants to provide products and services and, if applicable, get revenues in return. Figure 72 shows popular ways of utilization of IP in the software industry. The obious case is that the software vendor licenses software directly to the customer by granting usage rights. A second case is that the software vendor engages with a reseller. The software vendor grants sublicensing rights to the reseller and the reseller licenses the software to his customer by granting usage rights. In addition, the software vendor can grant licenses to patents held by the software vendor to patent licensees.

Foundations of the software business and their relevance for due diligence

Utilization of intellectual property (Examples)

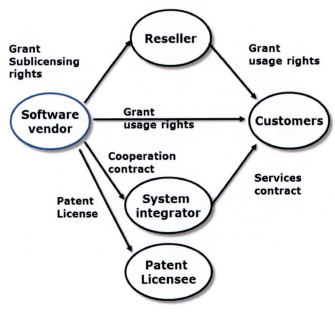

© Dr. Karl Popp 2012

Figure 72: Utilization of IP

Example

The software vendor in Figure 72 needs distribution and sublicensing rights for the software products delivered to Customers and Reseller. As part of the cooperation contract, the System Integrator might have rights to get a demo version of the software, so the software vendor needs rights to be able to do that, too.

Utilizations and impact on IPR review

For all intended utilizations, the corresponding rights needed for all utilizations have to be available to the software vendor. That means that the software vendors has to have appropriate rights for each and every com-

Foundations of the software business and their relevance for due diligence

ponent of the software product to execute each and every intended utilization.

Key questions Utilization

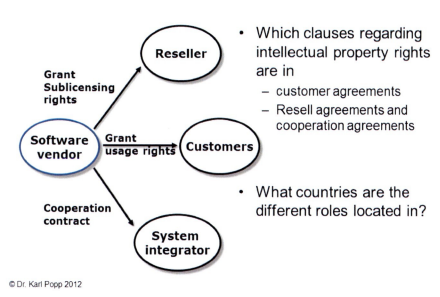

© Dr. Karl Popp 2012

Figure 73: Key questions on utilization of IP

So important requirements for the review of intellectual property come from the utilizations. The next steps is to find the intellectual property used as part of the review of status and usage of IP rights.

Review of own intellectual property and intellectual property used

Here you examine how intellectual property was created, acquired or licensed in the software company along the following questions:

☐ Has the target sufficiently taken measures that work results of employees and service providers are IP that is owned by the target?

Page 155

☐ Which patents, trademarks, copyrights, title protection, competition law and subsidiary measures exist and have been taken by the target?

☐ Which clauses regarding intellectual property rights are in customer and cooperation agreements to ensure that no intellectual property or trade secrets are "lost"?

☐ Which third party intellectual property (e.g. Open Source Software) was and is used by the target and does the target have the appropriate usage rights fitting the utilizations?

Key questions Sources 1

© Dr. Karl Popp 2012

Figure 74: Key questions on sources of IP 1

For each of its supplier relationships, the software vendor must ensure that it

☐ Either owns the intellectual property, which he uses or

Foundations of the software business and their relevance for due diligence

☐ has sufficient rights to use third-party IPR that are in compliance with the intended utilizations.

Usage rights of third party intellectual property rights are e.g.:

☐ Licenses for patents held by other companies,

☐ Rights to use software components owned by other companies,

☐ Rights to use open source software and freeware, which usually are available under open source and freeware licenses.

Key questions Sources 2

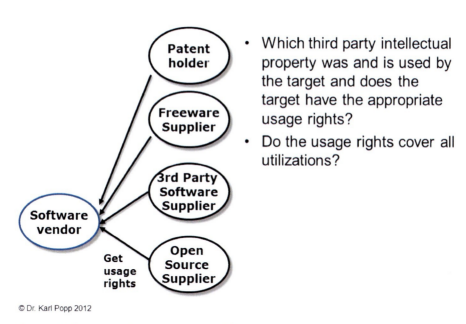

- Which third party intellectual property was and is used by the target and does the target have the appropriate usage rights?
- Do the usage rights cover all utilizations?

© Dr. Karl Popp 2012

Figure 75: Key questions on sources of IP 2

Foundations of the software business and their relevance for due diligence

Recommendation

For ensuring open source license compliance I recommend Black Duck. Black Duck offers solutions and services to quickly find, identify and assess the quality of open source code as part of a due diligence scan.

Deal breakers regarding IP

Deal breakers in the software industry regarding IP are often:

☐ Missing rights to use patents that are critical to business success,

☐ Missing patents for target inventions,

☐ The target is subject to or in danger of litigations,

☐ Barriers for the utilization of IP exist, that endanger the business success or

☐ The target violates IP rights of other companies.

If at all possible, you should have the target resolve these issues pre close. If they cannot be resolved, you might want to walk away from the deal.

SOFTWARE-IP.COM website

This is your go-to site for all wisdom in intellectual property topics relating to software.
http://www.software-ip.com

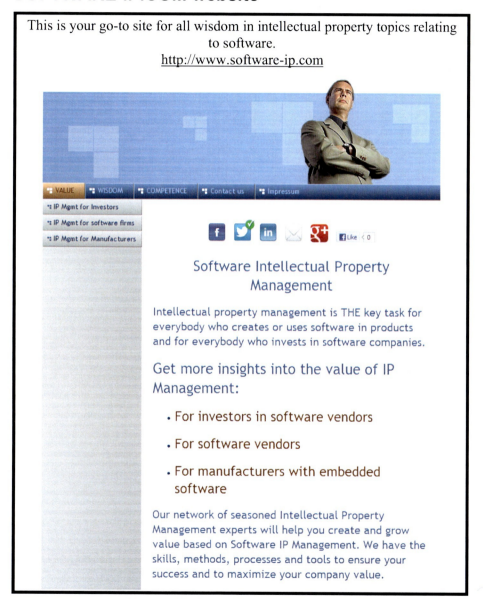

VALUE   WISDOM   COMPETENCE   Contact us   Impressum

: IP Mgmt for Investors

: IP Mgmt for software firms

: IP Mgmt for Manufacturers

Software Intellectual Property Management

Intellectual property management is THE key task for everybody who creates or uses software in products and for everybody who invests in software companies.

Get more insights into the value of IP Management:

- For investors in software vendors

- For software vendors

- For manufacturers with embedded software

Our network of seasoned Intellectual Property Management experts will help you create and grow value based on Software IP Management. We have the skills, methods, processes and tools to ensure your success and to maximize your company value.

Foundations of the software business and their relevance for due diligence

6.6 Business model risks in the software industry

In other sections of this book we have learned about the software business and its specifics. Here, we look at popular risk related to business models in software companies and merger integrations of software companies. We look at three business model archetypes, Lessor, Creator and Contractor.

Chances and risks of software business models

Business Model	Chances	Risks
Inventor	Monetizing intellectual property	Safeguarding and defending IP
Lessor	Growing license revenues	Revenue does not scale
Contractor	Growing service revenues	Cost too high, quality issues

© Dr. Karl Popp 2013

Figure 76: Risks in software business models

Risks in three business model archetypes

The *Inventor* business model archetype creates software. For inventors it is critical to monetize on the intellectual property that is created. Popular risks are IP infringement and loss of IP as well as the open source and third party license compliance risk that we already mentioned

Foundations of the software business and their relevance for due diligence

Lessor business needs growth of license revenue. So a key risk found in many deals is that the revenue does not scale post close.

Contractors provide services to customers and they would like to grow service revenues. Typical risks are that the cost are too high and quality might not be good enough.

Since most software vendors have a hybrid business model containing Lessor, Creator and Contractor, they are all likely to have all the risk mentioned above.

Mitigation of these risks

How do I protect me from these risks, how do I cope with these risks?

For the inventor business it is paramount that intellectual property is created, documented and protected. Copyright protection is not enough. You certainly should patent key inventions to protect them and to proof you invented it in case of litigation. The resulting portfolio of intellectual property should be managed using IP Management. See http://www.softwareipmanagement.com for details.

Mitigation of business model risk

Business Model	Risks	Risk Mitigation
Inventor	Safeguarding and defending IP	IP Management
Lessor	Revenue does not scale	Early, detailed revenue planning and revenue commitments
Services	Cost too high, quality issues	Detailed planning and early implementation of scalable model for services

© Dr. Karl Popp 2013

Figure 77: Mitigating risks of business model archetypes

Protection for the lessor business: you should do early, detailed revenue planning in the due diligence phase and create a plan of all steps needed to be prepared to create the revenue including staffing.

The two risks of the Contractor business can be mitigated as follows.

Plan to establish a scalable Contractor business which wil be implemented to run the services. Plan to have enough well educated people in the right location and geography at the right time to grow your Contractor business without sacrificing quality.

6.7 Takeaways from chapter 6

We have defined and analysed business models and revenue models in the software industry in this chapter and have mentioned impact on due

Foundations of the software business and their relevance for due diligence

diligence. With intellectual property being one of the key assets in the software industry, we have learned about how to conduct intellectual property due diligence. One section of this chapter looked at specific risks of business models that are popular in the software industry.

Foundations of the software business and their relevance for due diligence

DRKARLPOPP.COM Software business videos

Based on many presentations on the software business, i have started to pre-pare videos on many topics like software business models, software revenue models, goals of software vendors for their partner ecosystems and many more. The objective is to provide software business education for software executives online at
http://www.drkarlpopp.com/softwareecosystemvideos.html..

Here are some examples for video lessons:

 Lecture 1
Business Model Basics

 Lecture 2
Revenue models in the software industry

 Lecture 3
Open Source Business Models

 Lecture 4
Software supply chains: Overview

 Lecture 5
Software supplier relationships: OEM,Resell,etc.

Software business education using videos is cheap, convenient and effective. Please use the link below to access the videos. Try them today!

You can find my software business education videos on
http://www.drkarlpopp.com/softwareecosystemvideos.html.

Foundations of the software business and their relevance for due diligence

7. Foundations of software ecosystems and their relevance for due diligence

In due diligence we have to look at the ecosystem of the target to make sure we understand and analyze the ecosystem, decide about the future ecosystem strategy and plan merger integration activities accordingly. From the acquirer's point of view we might look at overlaps with existing partnerships and ecosystems, consolidation needs, new business models for partnerships to be created etc.

You can read a lot of articles today talking about a competition of ecosystems and how large software vendors are trying to build ecosystems around themselves. But what is an ecosystem in this space, how does it work, what are the benefits to software vendors and members of the ecosystem?

In this section we focus on ecosystems that form around a software vendor. So why is it interesting to look at such an ecosystem? As a software vendor you can influence, participate in and leverage the ecosystem for your purposes. **Leveraging the ecosystem** for a software vendor might mean

- ❐ to **outsource** certain activities like programming or testing or selling to other members of the ecosystem;

- ❐ To **generate revenue** from the ecosystem, e.g. by having partners sell your software or getting a share of the partner's revenue for endorsing his software;

- ❐ To create **network effects**, e.g. by leveraging a customer community by having satisfied customers attract new customers by acting as a reference for your solutions;

- ❐ To let the ecosystem do most of the **innovation** on your platform. In fact, the innovation created by the ecosystem is important for the software vendor because the innovation power of the total ecosystem is much bigger and has much more diversity than the software vendor itself.

Example

Just remember the many applications available for the Apple iPhone. What Apple did was creating standardized interfaces to products to attract other software vendors to build (and integrate) complementing products. This creates and grows the market for complementing products and the underlying platform. This might also increase lock-in of your customers with the platform.

Looking at real life examples in a later chapter, we will find out that different vendors have different goals in leveraging the ecosystem and that different vendors are in different stages of maturity in managing and leveraging their ecosystem. But let us start with looking at some fundamentals of ecosystems for software vendors. Parts of this chapter relate to the great research done by Iansiti and Levien [IaLe04].

7.1   Natural Ecosystems

What is the origin of the term ecosystem and how can we leverage existing research on natural ecosystems to draw conclusions for ecosystems of companies?

Definition of natural ecosystems

The term ecosystem originates from research about natural ecosystems. Researchers define an ecosystem as a bordered part of nature, where a large number of elements (e.g. plants, animals) are under consideration. The elements in the ecosystem are interacting in a number of ways. Examples of interaction are an animal eating a plant or a small fish cleaning the skin of a large fish.

Now let us review the results of this research and how we can use these results to look at ecosystems of software companies.

Foundations of software ecosystems and their relevance for due diligence

Structural properties of ecosystems

Important structural properties of natural ecosystems are: Elements, Relationships, Structure, Boundaries, Openness and Hubs.

Elements: as mentioned before, elements in natural ecosystems are usually plants or animals.

Relationships: there can be direct or indirect relationships between the elements of an ecosystem. A simple example for a relationship is a food chain where one species serves as prey to another species.

Complex structure: In nature we may find ecosystems with a complex structure. They have such a magnitude of elements as well as a magnitude of direct and indirect relationships that it is often impossible to describe the ecosystem as a whole. For that reason, often only a subset of elements and relationships will be used to build a model of the ecosystem. That can be done by abstraction or by setting artificial boundaries of the ecosystem.

So the easy way to analyze an ecosystem is to take some elements and study their direct relationships only. But there is a caveat: since natural ecosystems have many direct and indirect relationships between their elements and the effect of the indirect relationships might be stronger than the direct effects, this model will likely be inappropriate to study the behavior of an ecosystem.

Boundaries: Boundaries can be natural boundaries, like the shoreline of a lake, or artificial boundaries which are drawn to keep the size of the ecosystem under consideration manageable. In natural ecosystems it is often hard to draw a natural boundary to an ecosystem, since elements interact with the outside world and elements react to the outside world.

Openness: although an ecosystem has borders, it is an open system, which means it has relationships beyond the boundaries to the outside world. This means the outside world can influence, disturb or send new elements to the ecosystem and vice versa.

Foundations of software ecosystems and their relevance for due diligence

Hubs: Research across numerous different types of ecosystems shows that often a small number of elements exist, that have a much higher number of relationships than the other elements of the ecosystem. These elements are called hubs. Hubs can have a positive impact on the stability of an ecosystem by being robust against external effects.

Behavior properties of an ecosystem

How does an ecosystem change, how does it react to external effects, what are its behavior properties overall? This is what we are looking at in this section.

Reactions of ecosystems

Based on an exogenous impulse, ecosystems might react unpredictably and non-linearly. This makes it hard to analyze the behaviour of an ecosystem.

For managing ecosystems using exogenous impulses, this means that impulses have to be applied carefully to see what the impact of the impulse will be.

Self-organization

Natural ecosystems are self-organizing. That means elements of an ecosystem start building relationships and interact with other elements independent of external effects on the ecosystem. In essence, this means that a new ecosystem is built without an external leader or orchestrator. It is also important to note the self-organization is an ongoing process. New relationships are built and old ones disappear over time.

Adaptability

Change inside and outside the ecosystem happens. Change in an ecosystem can mean a variety of things: a change in the number of elements or a change in the natural habitat of the elements.

Foundations of software ecosystems and their relevance for due diligence

The elements of the ecosystem as well as the whole ecosystem are able to adapt to changes. Change in an ecosystem can mean a variety of things: a change in the number of elements or a change in the natural habitat of the elements.

Stability

Although natural ecosystems often seem to be fragile, they often exhibit an astonishing stability against changes in the ecosystem and from the outside world. This is due to a number of intertwined regulating bio mechanisms that exist in the ecosystem. As mentioned before, hubs have a positive impact on stability.

Two specific kinds of stabilities are discussed in literature, resistance and resilience.

Resistance is the ability of an ecosystem to fend off external disturbances and invasions into the ecosystem.

Resilience is the ability of ecosystems to return to its original state after an exogenous shock had occurred and the velocity of this adaption.

Co-evolution

The different elements in an ecosystem are dependent on each other in some way. Evolution of one element takes place influenced by the evolutionary changes in another related element. So the different elements co-evolve.

Behavior of single elements of the ecosystem

Behavior of elements is a key factor in the attempt to describe the behavior of the whole ecosystem. Behavior of an element is influenced by the experience of the element in similar situations and its strategy. Elements of natural ecosystems often have a memory and their behavior is influenced by their history, this is especially true with animals and human beings.

Regarding strategies, research on natural ecosystems found three particular strategies that are found in natural ecosystems: Dominator, Niche player and Keystone player. As we will see later on, these strategies can also be found in economic ecosystems.

Keystone players

Keystone players are vital elements of natural ecosystems. They usually are hubs and they are encouraging the health of the ecosystem by supporting the health of other elements of the ecosystem. It is important to notice, that it is not the size of a keystone, but only the sheer number of relationships and its behavior that make it a keystone. Keystones are exhibiting the following behaviors:

- ❏ defeating of dominants and competitors,

- ❏ mutualism, i.e. they directly support niche players and leave niches unoccupied,

- ❏ system enabling, i.e. enabling exchange between elements.

Keystones support the health of other elements of the ecosystem. By doing this, they also ensure their own survival.

Example

Good Examples of companies behaving as keystone players are large software vendors. They are acting as a keystone in their partner ecosystems. The best example is Microsoft. They foster their partners by providing them with cheap development licenses and marketing help as well as a channel to reach customers via Microsoft's online partner marketplace.

The flipside of keystones is that if a keystone player is removed from an ecosystem, the ecosystem can be severely damaged.

Niche players

Niche players occupy niches in the ecosystem by specializing and differentiating themselves from other members of the ecosystem. Each niche player has limited reach and impact on the ecosystem. They are neither dominators nor keystone players. A niche player usually is weaker than a dominator and smaller in size. So a niche player must be aware of the dominators and keystones in the network to survive.

While the importance of a single niche player for the ecosystem is limited, most of the members of ecosystems are niche players and niche players also provide diversity in an ecosystem.

Dominators

A Dominator is pretty much the opposite of a keystone. A dominator leverages a critical position in the ecosystem to exploit or take over a large portion of the ecosystem.

If a dominator progressively takes over the ecosystem by occupying an ever growing number of niches, this is called physical domination.

As you can see, dominators typically damage the health of the ecosystem.

When analyzing ecosystem roles, the acquirer has to determine the target's role in its different ecosystems and to anticipate and plan for changes in ecosystem strategy and operations. In post merger integration, the strategy and operations changes are executed. The effects of changing ecosystem strategies can be dramatic, like e.g. all participants leaving the ecosystem or all participants being reluctant to changes. Another dramatic example is the acquisition of a niche player by a dominator. The question arises what the effect on the niche player's ecosystem are. Try to anticipate the changes, analyze the consequences and plan activities for post merger integration accordingly.

Foundations of software ecosystems and their relevance for due diligence

7.2   Economic Ecosystems

Based on the terminology and the knowledge about natural ecosystems, we will now investigate economic ecosystems.

Definition of economic ecosystems

An economic **ecosystem** is a set of companies that exchange products or services to serve a common goal or to achieve higher levels of individual goals. Often companies in an ecosystem are aligned along value chains, where each of the steps of the value chain adds value to the goods and services and provides them to the next step of the value chain. Or ecosystems form around a value chain that serves the same set of customers, e.g. the customers of a large software vendor like Microsoft or SAP.

Example

Members of the ecosystem of an industrial manufacturing company are material supplier companies, customers and the manufacturing company itself. They are aligned along the supplier-manufacturer-customer value chain.

Structure of economic ecosystems

Until now, we often used structural depictions of ecosystems, so here is a more formal definition of the structural elements of economic ecosystems:

Elements: Companies (or legal entities) are the elements in an economic ecosystem.

Relationships: Relationships are defined by the exchange of products and services and compensating exchanges of products and services. So companies provide products or services which are consumed by other companies. The provisioning of products and services is compensated by providing products, services or payments.

Boundaries: As in natural ecosystems, boundaries of economic ecosystems are hard to establish. In a networked global economy, ecosystems

Foundations of software ecosystems and their relevance for due diligence

go beyond traditional industry boundaries and even beyond country and regional boundaries.

Openness: Economic Ecosystems are open, just like natural ecosystems.

Behavior of economic ecosystems

The core of the behavior of economic ecosystems is around the exchange of goods and services and all the interaction that is needed to coordinate this exchange. While it is easy to describe the behavior of one company, it is not that easy to describe the behavior of an economic ecosystem. The key aspects of behavior are: self-organization, adaptability, stability and co-evolution.

Self-organization: An ecosystem will develop around a software vendor even if the software vendor will not actively spark it. Usually there is at least one company for every niche, that promises an opportunity to run a profitable business. So there should be at least one company for every niche in the ecosystem around a software vendor.

Adaptability: As with natural ecosystems, economic ecosystems are adaptive. They frequently react to changes in the behavior of competitors, customers, partners and the general economic environment. Changes can occur in

☐ The macro-economic environment, like taxes, export laws or competition regulations as well as macroeconomic parameters like GDP growth;

☐ The micro-economic environment, like new or changing customer, supplier or partner demands as well as new competitors;

☐ Technology, like changing or new technology or process innovation.

Stability: Keeping an economic ecosystem stable under the changes of the economic environment is a challenge to companies. The adaptability of an economic ecosystem is a key prerequisite to stability. Conditions for reaching a stable equilibrium after an external effect has been studied on a macro-economic level, but there is little information on stability and equilibriums in economic ecosystems.

Co-evolution: Evolution of one company affects the evolution of another company. Examples are the evolution of operating systems, the evolution of databases, middleware and applications on software vendors using these platforms.

Example

Co-evolution is an ongoing task in the software industry. If a software vendor offers a solution based on Microsoft Windows, the software vendor's products have to evolve with the evolution of Microsoft Windows. That means that the software vendor's have to be available on currently supported versions of Windows, the customers have to run current versions of Windows etc.

Strategies in economic ecosystems

Ecosystem strategy defines how a company will deal with its ecosystem. Three specific strategies are popular in ecosystem literature: dominators, keystone players and niche players.

Niche players

In economic ecosystems, most companies follow a niche player strategy. So they focus their business on critical competencies in narrow areas of expertise, if there is an opportunity to run a profitable business. They usually are smaller companies and they usually outnumber other strategies in an ecosystem. Niche players should find suitable ways to co-develop with other companies.

Dominators

The behaviour of dominators was already explained above. Especially in ecosystems that are impacted by fast technological changes, a dominator strategy is a questionable strategy. A dominator has to provide all the innovation in all areas he is covering. He has to take all the cost of innovation and he does not have the diversity and evolutionary power that is created by an ecosystem. In addition, there is the assumption, that the ability to provide innovation decreases with the size of a dominator company.

Besides acquisition or destruction of companies, a dominator can exploit an economic ecosystem. Exploitation can be in the form of value domination, where the dominator drains all the value from the ecosystem.

While there are positive economic aspects of domination in the short term, like standardization of markets for complements, there are clearly negative aspects in the long term. These are decreasing diversity of the ecosystem, decreasing innovation rate and resistance from regulatory authorities to the power of the dominator in its market.

Keystone players

Keystone players behave in favour of other players, esp. by protecting niche players.

Why is protecting niche players important for an ecosystem? It is because the number and diversity of niche players also determines the speed and diversity of innovation in an economic ecosystem, which is an important prerequisite for the success of an ecosystem.

Since keystone players are important for an ecosystem to adapt to change according to the literature, they are even more important in rapidly changing economic ecosystems. They enable the diversity in an ecosystem by helping niche players to settle in the ecosystem and by protecting the niches against dominators.

Keystones are the engine of evolution and innovation in an ecosystem. Products are constantly recombined to provide an ever renewing product and service offerings. For technology related ecosystems, this effect of keystones is a key success factor for survival and adaptability of the overall ecosystem.

Evolution of economic ecosystems

A software vendor who wants to change his ecosystem will do this by co-evolution of the players in the ecosystem. The software vendor will change (evolve) his behaviour to trigger the evolution of partner behaviour. And the software vendor certainly has to co-evolve with changing behaviour of its partners.

Example

One example is that the software vendor changes its partner program, e.g. by increasing fees for the partner programs. Partners will co-evolve with that strategy change (adapt to higher pricing) or they will not adapt to the change in partner programs (walk away).

Another example is a software vendor (Microsoft) that offered on premise solutions in the past is changing its offering to on demand services and the partner ecosystem has to adapt to that strategy change.

Remember that the behaviour of complex ecosystems is hard to predict. This will especially be relevant if there are changes that have a negative impact on the partners in the ecosystem. One example would be that the software vendor massively increases fees for partner programs. Partners might adapt to that or they might decide to leave the ecosystem.

> To manage the impact of changes to an economic ecosystem, we should always plan for stepwise evolutionary changes, that are communicated early and directly to partners before executing the changes.

7.3   Software Ecosystem Overview

A **Software Ecosystem** is an economic ecosystem that forms around one specific software vendor. As the software industry changes rapidly, research presented earlier shows, that the success of a software vendor is not only defined by its own success but by the success of its ecosystem.

This seems to be true, no matter if the software vendor acts as niche player, dominator or keystone.

The companies in the **software ecosystem** interact with the software vendor or its customers or partners in the following ways:

☐ they **sell products or services to the software vendor's customers**. These products or services might be related to or integrated with the software vendor's products or services,

☐ they **sell the software vendor's products**, e.g. as **Value Added Resellers** (VAR),

☐ they **sell services to the software vendor**, to the customers or to the software vendor's partners,

☐ they **license or subscribe to the software vendor's products** for internal use or for inclusion in own products,

☐ they **license software to the software vendor** (suppliers),

☐ they **align on standards** with the software vendor to create bigger markets based on standardized products or

☐ And last but not least, companies can sell intellectual property to the software vendor. That means they are potential **candidates for acquisition** or IP purchase by the software vendor.

As a result, Figure 78 shows the players in the ecosystem of the software vendor. Since all companies selling products to the software vendor's customers are part of the software vendor's ecosystem, the competitors of the software vendor are also part of the ecosystem. Companies might even decide to work together with a competitor in a specific market segment. This is called co-opetition.

Foundations of software ecosystems and their relevance for due diligence

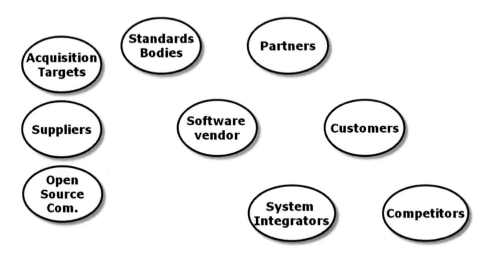

Figure 78: Players in the software ecosystem

Example

> *For software vendor SAP, examples for the different roles are Oracle (competitor and supplier of database software), Maxware (acquisition target), IBM Global Services (System Integrator), Siemens (customer and partner), Object Management Group (standards body).*

Consider the impact of ecosystems being merged or consolidated. Eco-system partners have to adapt to the change, which might not only be a change in strategy but also a change in contracts. Will the participants of the ecosystem adapt or leave? A question for post merger integration would be: if you have 200 partners of the target and you must change all these contracts, who will execute these changes and in which timeframe?

Foundations of software ecosystems and their relevance for due diligence

7.4   Types of Software Ecosystems

Usually the software vendor applies different strategies and tactics for different parts of the software ecosystem. These strategies and tactics must be aligned with the business model. Figure 79 shows the different types of ecosystems that are typically addressed separately by a software vendor.

First and foremost, there is the **customer ecosystem**. It contains existing and potential customers of the software vendor.

Then there is the **partner ecosystem**, which contains the software partners and the system integrators. An often neglected, but important ecosystem is the ecosystem of suppliers.

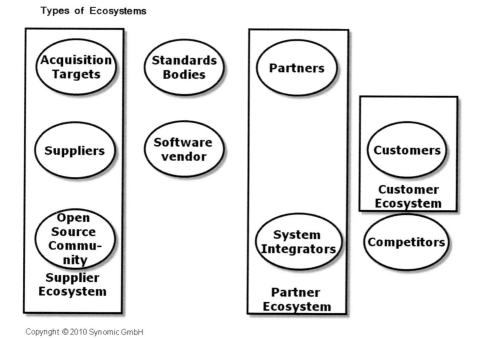

Copyright © 2010 Synomic GmbH

Figure 79: Types of Ecosystems

Foundations of software ecosystems and their relevance for due diligence

7.5 Software Ecosystem Goals

Let us have a look at the typical **goals** of a software vendor for the ecosystem activities. Usually a software vendor's ecosystem activities are targeted at one or several of the following goals: Financial, customer related, product related, network effect related and market related goals.

In due diligence, we analyze the ecosystems of the target, compare it to the ecosystem and ecosystem strategy of the acquirer and plan integration efforts accordingly. After the following overview, we will provide details for each of the goals.

Financial goals

❏ Monetize on the ecosystem

❏ Save cost

Customer related goals

❏ Attract new customers

❏ Increase the stickiness of solutions (and vendor lock-in of customers)

❏ Make every partner a customer

Product related goals

❏ Strengthen market presence

❏ Strengthen software vendor's offerings

❏ Innovate and co-innovate solutions

Network effect related goals

❏ Maximize ecosystem gravity

❏ Maximize retention in the ecosystem

Foundations of software ecosystems and their relevance for due diligence

Market related goals

❏ Standardize markets

❏ Extend market reach

❏ Establish competition in service markets

❏ Create new markets and communities

Financial goals

Now let us see more details on the financial goals for software ecosystems.

Monetize on the ecosystem

Monetizing on the ecosystem means **creating or increasing revenue streams** by leveraging the ecosystem. Revenue streams can come from partner program and community fees and increased product revenue due to positive sales effects from the ecosystem. Figure 80 shows some examples of revenue streams to be created or increased in an ecosystem.

Engagement between partners can be adhoc, like a one-off resell agreement to serve a single customer, or it can be formalized, like a partner program offered by one of the software vendors. Or it can be a resell contract with committed resources on both sides and marketing budget and a revenue plan.

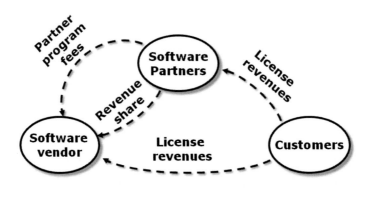

Revenue streams in the ecosystem

Figure 80: Examples of revenue streams in the ecosystem

Partner program fees are the entry ticket fees for partners into partner programs. The tricky thing is: if the fees are higher than the anticipated value of the benefits, partners will not join the partner program. So software vendors should carefully define and handle fees associated with the partner programs to make sure partners are not deterred from joining the partner programs.

Product revenue from the ecosystem can come from the partner ecosystem providing revenue streams from reselling your products or from services fees or from license fees for using your products or from revenue shares. We will dig deeper into these matters later in this book. Software partners can also help increase license revenue from customers by promoting the software vendor´s solution in a new market or industry.

Foundations of software ecosystems and their relevance for due diligence

Example

A simple, but powerful example for monetizing the ecosystem is Microsoft's ecosystem for Microsoft Windows and Microsoft Office. These products generate significant revenue just because there is an enormous ecosystem of users and partners, which provide complementing products. So Microsoft behaves like a dominator to other software vendors offering operating systems, but like a keystone to software vendors building applications that are not in competition with Microsoft's line of products.

Please note that merger activities might have a significant impact on monetization in ecosystems. So you have to carefully predict the impact of the merger activity on your ecosystem monetizations.

Save cost

How can a software vendor save cost by leveraging the ecosystem? Cost savings mainly result from outsourcing the software vendor's activities to the ecosystem, from educating the ecosystem and from leveraging the ecosystem as multiplier for product knowledge.

Outsourcing to the community means that the community can take over tasks of the software vendor. The following tasks are usually (at least partially) outsourced to the community: presales activities, sales activities, product distribution, post-sales activities like support, answering product-related questions and providing additional, complementing products.

Example

Since Microsoft has outsourced large parts of their sales to partners, it is important for them to guide partners to sales opportunities. Microsoft has processes and tools in place to ensure that.

If you outsource, you have to make sure the ecosystem provides quality products and services to customers and prices are low. One way to establish that is that you let several partners enter the ecosystem and establish quality and price competition between the partners. Microsoft has done so by differentiating the partners based on their competencies and by ensuring quality by establishing certification programs for consultants, developers and partner solutions.

Education is done by providing software vendors and the partners' and customers' knowledge to the community and by enabling customers and partners to communicate with each other by using the community. This is usually done by creating online communities, which are websites, where members of the community can access and publish knowledge to the rest of the community.

Customer related goals

An ecosystem is a place for an existing customer or a prospect to build trust in the software vendor's solutions. Trust is also a key ingredient for customer retention. Trust is built between the customers and a software vendor by:

❏ The sheer number of participants in the ecosystem,

❏ The number of partners offering solutions and services for the software vendor's solutions,

❏ Information from existing customers shared in the ecosystem.

Attract new customers

Customer communities can start a viral effect to attract new customers. This happens when existing customers spread the news about their use of solutions or when the lock-in of existing customers extends to the customer's ecosystem of suppliers and customers. The reason is simple: to lower the integration cost between suppliers, the customer and the customer's customer it makes sense to use identical technology and applications. If the customer has enough market power, he might even force its suppliers and customers to use identical technology and applications.

Increase the stickiness of solutions (and vendor lock-in of customers)

With a high number of partner solutions based on or integrated with the software vendor´s solutions, the stickiness of the software vendor´s solution increases. This means that the **switching cost** for the customer to switch to a competitor´s solution increases. But beware: this is only true, if the interface between the partner solution and the software vendor´s solution is not sufficiently standardized.

Example

There are thousands of partner solutions running on Microsoft Windows. Imagine a company who has 50 Windows-based solutions running. For that company, the switching cost to switch to another operating system is very high. It might even be impossible to switch to Linux if the Windows-based solutions do not have identical substitutes on Linux. There are so many Windows based computers in our economy; Hal Varian speaks of "societal lock-in".

Make every partner a customer

How do you easily increase the number of customers by leveraging partners? You make every partner a customer. Sounds simple, in some cases it is. Microsoft offers attractive packages of its products to partners for internal use.

Since many partners use some Microsoft technology anyway for internal use, this offer comes in handy and Microsoft increases its footprint in partners acting as customers. It also increases the lock-in of partners to the Microsoft products and platforms.

Product related goals

These are the goals related to products and services:

Foundations of software ecosystems and their relevance for due diligence

Strengthen market presence

Software vendors can choose diversified partnership strategies for regional and local markets. They do so by leveraging the software partners market expertise, market access as well as access to new and existing customer accounts. The partnership strategies differ by presence and strength of the software vendor and its partners in the specific markets. Let us have a look at an example from SAP to make it clear.

Example

In Asia, SAP partners aggressively to capture larger parts of the Asian market. So partnerships target increased market share in Asia. Strong partners in Asia can increase the growth rate for SAP in this region.

In Europe, with its strong presence and market saturation in large accounts, SAP partners to capture additional revenue in existing accounts or to capture larger market shares in industries, where SAP sees growth potential. This means, that partnerships in EMEA target new revenue streams.

Strengthen software vendor´s offerings

The portfolio of solutions of a software vendor always has whitespaces and adjacent, complementing solutions, which are not offered by the software vendor itself. Complementing offerings from partners can be positioned in these whitespaces or adjacent areas. This leads to a more complete solution offering for the customers, combining the software vendor's products with partner products. This might lead to a customer perception of a complete offering for the customer´s business problem.

Example

Oracle resells IDS Scheer´s ARIS Product Suite as part of its Business Process Analysis Suite. Goal of this relationship is to complete the ra-

Foundations of software ecosystems and their relevance for due diligence

*ther technical Oracle offering with proven business modeling capabil-
ities from IDS Scheer (now owned by Software AG).*

The business relationship between the software vendors and its partners
can take many shapes, which are discussed in chapter 7.10.

Innovate and co-innovate solutions

A sound innovation strategy of a software vendor contains a mix of internal and external innovation. External innovation happens outside of
the company walls of the software vendor, mainly by partners, but also
by customers and system integrators. Co-innovation means that two
companies are working together to innovate.

A partner can build a solution based on a software vendor's platform or
solutions. In this case, the engineering work and cost resides with the
partner. Software vendors usually provide some sort of certification to
prove the interoperability of the solutions. There is more detail in chapter
8.9.

Two Software vendors can also work together to innovate. This is often
done by defining development work for both software vendors and by
providing an interface between the respective solutions. There is more
detail in chapter 8.10 how this type of partnership is defined.

Network effect related goals

Ecosystems can be used to fight competitors. The reasoning behind that
is based on network effects. The **network effect** says that the value of a
product increases with the number of customers of that product.

Example

*A very good example for a network effect is the software-based tele-
phone service Skype. Skype offers free telephone calls between users
of Skype. The more people use Skype, the higher the value for each of
the Skype users.*

Foundations of software ecosystems and their relevance for due diligence

Network effects can be direct or indirect. A **direct network effect** comes from compatibility between products. Within a network of customers, all customers using the same software have low integration cost.

Example

Examples for direct network effects are low integration cost for different companies using the same software from SAP or from Microsoft. Another example is the success of the Portable Document Format (PDF) from Adobe. The fact that Adobe Reader was available at no charge laid the foundation to the widespread adoption of the PDF format.

An **indirect network effect** comes from the assumption that widespread adoption of a product also leads to a large number of adjacent solutions and partners.

More customers and more partners in your ecosystem make it harder for a competitor to compete against you.

For customers, a large ecosystem of customers and partners

❒   provides a variety of solutions with low integration cost, which is application to application integration cost and

❒   promises low interoperability costs since integration cost for two customers using the same software is minimal. This is about business to business integration cost.

In an extreme case a competitor would have to pay customers money to adopt his products in favor of a company that has a large ecosystem and promises high gains for the customers from the network effect.

Example

One example for a software vendor wanting to exploit network effects is SAP buying Ariba. The idea is to provide integration between SAP and Ariba solutions and leverage the network effects within the Ariba customer network to sell SAP solutions.

Foundations of software ecosystems and their relevance for due diligence

In due diligence, consider the impact of the acquisition on network effects, which can be positive or negative. Looking again at a dominator buying a niche player, the customer and partner ecosystem might react negatively. This has to be taken into account when defining the ecosystem strategy and ecosystem-related activities for the post merger integration phase. As mentioned before, communication to partners is key.

Maximize ecosystem gravity

Maximizing the gravity of the ecosystem means increasing the number of participants in the ecosystem. The hope is that the more gravity the ecosystem has, the more it attracts new members for the ecosystem. Let's have a look at two ecosystem examples what this means for the software vendor.

Customer ecosystem gravity is measured by the number of customers in the ecosystem. A large customer ecosystem has a lot of advantages, from generating license and maintenance revenue to providing references and pilot customers. A large customer ecosystem can lead to a positive network effect, such that partners and customers of an existing customer might become a customer as well, based on the positive experience of the existing customer.

Partner ecosystem gravity is measured by the number of partners in an ecosystem. Especially for large software vendors like IBM, Microsoft, SAP and Oracle the ecosystem strategy is an important ingredient in the competitive strategy. On one hand, these big software vendors try to engage as many partners as possible; on the other hand they try to get the focus of the partner on their products, not on the competitor's products.

Typical measures to maximize ecosystem gravity are: installing network effects, maximizing the perceived value of ecosystem participation and keeping the entry barriers to the ecosystem low.

Foundations of software ecosystems and their relevance for due diligence

Example

Microsoft has the goal: Make partnering with Microsoft easy. So the entry barriers to become an entry level partner (called Registered Partner) are very low (just enter your data on a website) and there are no fees attached with this partnership. There is an additional incentive to enter this partnership: each partner gets a cheap package of licenses for Microsoft products. These activities serve additional goals: make every partner a customer and maximize retention in the ecosystem.

> In a perfect world, you might increase ecosystem gravity by merging two ecosystems of the acquirer and the target. In reality you have to analyse and respect the sentiment of the participants of both ecosystems to figure out what makes the merged ecosystem attractive to the participants.

Maximize retention of participants in the ecosystem

To maximize leverage of the ecosystem, it might make sense to attract as many participants as possible and to retain them. Retention of participants in the ecosystem is based on many factors. The most important factors are incentives and lock-in. Incentives for staying in the ecosystem are e.g. marketing opportunities and customer access for partners as well as a wide and attractive offering for customers in a vibrant ecosystem.

There are two ways to look at lock-in: partner and customer lock-in. Software vendors try to create partner lock-in by deepening the integration of partner solutions with the solutions of the software vendor. At the same time, the software vendor creates lock-in for customers that use the software vendor's solutions integrated with partner solutions.

Example

If a software vendor starts building an application on Microsoft Windows and the application grows over time, the software vendor might make use many of the Microsoft specific tools like Internet Explorer,

Sharepoint and Active Directory. This creates partner lock-in since it is high effort for the software vendor to switch e.g. to a Linux environment with different tools for web browsing, collaboration and identity management.

Market related goals

Software vendors try to influence and change markets with their ecosystem strategy. Standardizing markets, extending the market reach and creating new markets are good examples for a software vendor's goals relating to markets.

Standardize markets

One goal is important for software vendors: Homogenize the offering and the demand in a market. Markets can become more homogeneous by establishing standards. A common belief is that a more homogeneous market creates a bigger revenue opportunity for software vendors. But standardization often also lowers the entry barriers for new competitors and thus creates increased competition in this standardized market. Let's assume in a standardized market the competition and the market size grows. When does it make sense to create or enter a standardized market? It makes sense, if your market share is equal or larger in a standardized market.

Standardization can be driven by one or more vendors or by vendors, partners and customers alike. So either customers create a standardized demand for solutions or software vendors create a standardized offering.

Example

An interesting example for standardizing and growing markets is SAP's industry value network, where SAP, partners and customers work together to define and standardize features offered to customers in a specific vertical market. As soon as joint definitions exist from the customers and the software vendors, a standardized market is created.

Foundations of software ecosystems and their relevance for due diligence

Extend market reach

A software vendor can extend its market reach by leveraging partner's skills, knowledge and products as well as partner's market access and market coverage.

Let's have a look at market access and market coverage first: the partners' access to local, regional or vertical markets is a tempting business opportunity for a software vendor looking for partners.

The partners may position the software vendor's products in a certain market, they can refer customers from that market to the software vendor or they can act as a value added reseller to sell the software vendor's products into that specific market.

Example

Microsoft leverages its partner community to position Microsoft's horizontal partner offering in vertical markets. So Microsoft extends its market reach into verticals with these partnerships.

SAP leverages its partner community to sell into small and medium businesses. So SAP extends its market reach and breadth of channels into small and medium businesses.

Acquisitions and partner strategies often have one common goal that creates trouble: market extensions. Imagine a situation where an operating system vendor like Microsoft, with many partners building enterprise applications on the operating system. Microsoft acquired several companies building enterprise applications like Great Plains Software in 2001. The impact on the partner ecosystem is clear, Microsoft assimiliated an ecosystem space that was "reserved" for partners and on which partners built their revenue plans on.

So what about partners' skills, knowledge and products? Skills and knowledge can be leveraged in several ways. One common way for a software vendor is to leverage system integrators as partners for implementing solutions. This allows the software vendor to scale its solutions better than offering consulting services on its own.

Example

One limiting growth factor for SAP in the past was the availability of skilled consultants to implement SAP's solutions. So SAP got rid of this limiting growth factor by massively engaging with system integrators to provide "unlimited" resources for implementation of SAP solutions.

Create new markets and communities

As a software vendor you can even start a new ecosystem or make an existing ecosystem explicit and manage it under your leadership. Let us have a look at an example for creating a customer ecosystem.

Example

*In its effort to sell more software to business users, SAP has created the **business process expert community** (BPX). There are several positive effects of making this ecosystem explicit in an online community. SAP can listen and learn from the members of the customer and partner ecosystem and SAP can influence them and SAP can apply targeted marketing mechanisms at the business process expert community. In addition, the BPX members educate and give advice to each other, which lowers SAP's support cost.*

Foundations of software ecosystems and their relevance for due diligence

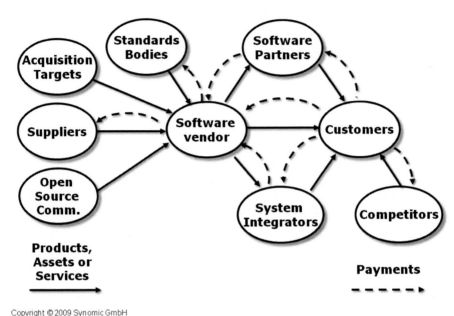

Figure 81: Exchange of products and services in the ecosystem

7.6 Exchange of goods and services in an ecosystem

How do the players in the ecosystem generate value? They do so by exchanging goods and services. Suppliers might license software to the software vendor, who pays for the license. The software vendor licenses software to the customers and so on. This leads to a spider web of goods, services and payments exchanged between the players of the ecosystem, as shown in Figure 81.

Example

In Figure 81 the software vendor might sell education services to the system integrator. Education services means training for consultants of the system integrator. The system integrator sells consulting services to the customer. The customer pays the system integrator service fees.

In due diligence, all relationships of the software vendor in Figure 81 have to be analyzed from a legal, operational and financial point of view. The acquirer has to determine if he intends to continue the relationships and if there have to be changes to the relationships, which again creates effort in post merger integration.

7.7 Roles of software companies in an ecosystem

Software Companies can take one or several different roles in the ecosystem depending on the goals they try to achieve. Figure 82 shows examples, which roles a software company can take: Supplier, Software Partner, Competitor, Customer and Acquisition Target.

Foundations of software ecosystems and their relevance for due diligence

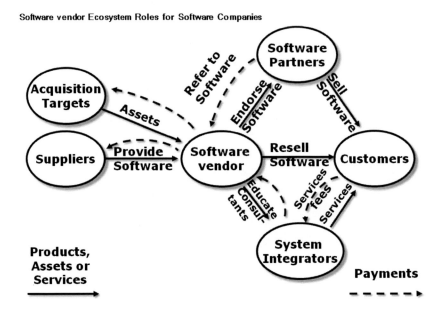

Figure 82: Roles in the ecosystem

In due diligence, we identify all applying roles for a software company and use role-specific due diligence activities for analysis.

Let us have a look at more details on the different roles.

Suppliers

A software vendor can act as a **supplier** to another software vendor. A supplier provides to the software vendor

☐ the right to use software for internal use or

☐ the right to redistribute or resell the software to customers or

☐ the right to include the software in one of the software vendor's offerings (open source or commercial license) or

Foundations of software ecosystems and their relevance for due diligence

❏   intellectual property (in the form of an IP purchase or by acquisition).

The right to include software in one of the software vendor´s offerings based on a commercial license is called **inbound OEM Software**. If OEM Software is provided free of charge, it is called **freeware**.

Looking deeper into the possible models for supplying software to a software vendor reveals the following models:

	Supplier	License fees	IP Risk	Support Risk
In-bound OEM	A Software vendor	Yes	Low	Low
Open Source	Open Source Community	No	High	High
Free-ware	A Software vendor	No	Medium	Medium
Resell	A Software vendor	Yes	Low	Low
Asset Deal	A Software vendor	No, but compensation for acquisition of IP	High	Low

Figure 83: Attributes of Supplier Relationships

In the case of **open source software**, the open source community supplies the software and a software vendor uses the software. The software vendor might also include and ship the open source software with its solutions. As shown in Figure 84, there is no license fee paid from the software vendor to the open source community. As every open source software comes with license terms, the software vendor has to conform to the license terms of the open source software used.

Foundations of software ecosystems and their relevance for due diligence

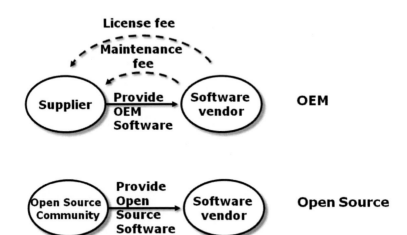

Figure 84: Supplier Roles OEM and Open Source

If the software vendor ships the open source software, the software vendor is responsible for support and maintenance of the software shipped, which includes the open source software. So the software vendor has to make sure he is able to support it.

Since compliance with the license terms of open source software used is important, help for doing that is available. One company specialized on analyzing open source usage and on analyzing the attached license terms is Black Duck. They offer a tool that automatically analyses the source code and determines the open source software used. Then you can determine if you can comply with the license terms and if you want to continue to use the open source software.

Foundations of software ecosystems and their relevance for due diligence

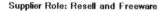

Supplier Role: Resell and Freeware

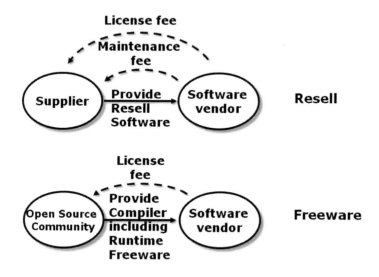

Figure 85: Supplier Roles Resell and Freeware

In due diligence, supplier due diligence is a key task. All supplier relationships are carefully analyzed from a contract point of view but also
from a risk and dependency point of view. For merger integration, corresponding mitigation activities are defined in due diligence. If there are
e.g. differences in service level agreements for product support in place
at the target and at the acquirer and the goal is to align them, you have to
align and adapt all supplier contracts as part of the merger integration
activities.

Software Partner

A software company can act as a **Partner** of the software vendor. Depending on how much the software vendor outsources to the partner,
there are different business models, processes and contracts.

Foundations of software ecosystems and their relevance for due diligence

Software company opportunities

In a software vendor´s ecosystem, you should try to leverage the relationships with other participants of the ecosystem. In general, your opportunities are to

❏ Tap into existing revenue streams,

❏ To create new revenue streams,

❏ To sell software and services to the software vendor, partners and customers,

❏ To leverage network effects and sell software and services to the customers´ and partners´ respective ecosystems.

Typically one of the following services is provided: generate leads for the software vendor, resell the software of the software vendor, and sell products which complement the software vendor´s products.

Software Partners

Software Partners are partners of the software vendor who are creating or selling software. They

❏ sell their software to customers,

❏ sell and distribute the software vendor´s products to customers,

❏ get their software endorsed to existing and potential customers of the software vendor,

❏ provide presales and sales services to the software vendor,

❏ provide post sales activities like service and support for the software vendor´s products to the customer or creation of customer references,

❏ get first mover advantage by co-innovating with the software vendor,

❏ get cheap licenses from software vendor,

❏ get financing from the software vendor,

❏   get marketing services from the software vendor.

The following matrix gives an overview of partnership models and the tasks of the software vendor that are outsourced to the software partner.

	Business Models			
	Revenue Share	Referral	OEM	Resell
Marketing	X	X	X	X
Lead genera-tion		X	X	X
Sales			X	X
Post sales			X	X
Service			X	X
Support			X	X
Maintenance			X	X

Figure 86: Business Models and outsourced tasks

Competitor

Software Companies can also become a **competitor** of another software vendor. Then all information about the rest of the ecosystem is important to know for the competitor. Why? Competition is not only about the customers, it is also about the partners and about how a software vendor manages and leverages the ecosystem. So be aware of the activities of competitors with their ecosystem.

Sometimes it makes sense to the software vendor to partner with competitors. In these special situations the upside of the partnership is perceived to be better than the downside of competition.

We might have significant impact of an acquisition on the competitive position and on the competitors of the acquirer and the target. You might get rid of some competitors due to the increase in the number of products and broadness of your portfolio, but you might also get on the radar of new competitors.

System Integrator

A **System Integrator** is a company that provides services to customers of software vendors. These services are focused on the implementation of the software vendor´s products and the integration of these products with other products the customer operates. In a nutshell a system integrator:

❑   sells implementation services to customers,

❑   sells software to customers.

What we mentioned for suppliers is also true for system integrator partnerships. In due diligence all contracts are reviewed and rated, in merger integration we might face numerous contract alignment and even termination activities. In addition we might need other system integrator partners, e.g. from the target´s partner ecosystem, to provide services for the newly acquired products and solutions.

It is also important to mention that all relationships to a system integrator have to be checked regarding the intellectual property related clauses in contracts.

Acquisition Target

Sometimes software companies become **acquisition targets** of a software vendor. If acquired, they would provide their assets to the software vendor for a financial compensation.

Visibility of a potential acquisition target to a software vendor might be created by participating in revenue generating partner programs of the software vendor. This is a perfect way to establish trust by showing that

Foundations of software ecosystems and their relevance for due diligence

the products are quality products and that the solution creates revenue in the software vendor´s customer base.

> Since there is a lot of M&A activity in the software industry, we check if there are former acquisitions that have been done by the acquisition target and look closely at the acquired product and the level of post merger integration that has happened. Often there are pending or open post merger integration tasks that the target has not executed on former acquisition targets. These tasks have to be considered when planning the post merger integration.

7.8   Online communities of users, customers and partners

Besides products, services and payments, information is also exchanged. Information is needed to make customers aware of products (marketing information), prepare the buying decision (product information or product quotes) and other information (product documentation or product reviews of customers and analysts). Information becomes especially important if a software vendor explicitly creates an **online community** of customers or partners. In such an online community information is exchanged between the software vendor and customers and partners, but also between the customers and between the partners.

Online communities are often managed communities, which mean that a software vendor has control over the community and leverages the community in a managed way.

Example

Examples for online communities are the SAP Developer Network (SDN), which is a large community of developers on the SAP platforms, and the Microsoft partner community.

Foundations of software ecosystems and their relevance for due diligence

> In due diligence, the target's communities are listed, analyzed and mirrored with the acquirer's existing communities. For merger integration, shut down of communities, consolidation of communities and of terms and conditions of community contracts may create massive workload.

7.9 Standards and Ecosystems

Standards in markets usually lower the thresholds for competitors to enter these markets. So standardization increases competition.

This is why large, predominant companies tend to limit standardization efforts to keep the thresholds for market entrants high.

At the same time, standardization might also result in market growth. This is where standardization becomes interesting. You basically trade an increased competition for a larger market. So the key decision is, if your revenue is bigger in a non-standardized market or in a standardized market.

If you are a software vendor and you have to decide about creating standards, you have to think about what your market share and revenue will be in a standardized market. If you can keep or increase your revenue in a standardized market, it certainly makes sense to go for standardization.

Standards leader

In standardization efforts, there is often one or more standards leaders. Standards leaders are companies that drive standardization forward. These standard leaders need supporters to create a standard which is accepted in the marketplace.

Standards for complements

Large software vendors often standardize interfaces of their solutions to allow third party software vendors to integrate their solutions. The intentions for the large software vendors are:

❑ Create a (larger) standardized market for complementing products,

❑ Let competition and certification drive prices of complementing products down and quality up,

❑ Create gravity for a technology platform like Microsoft Windows or SAP NetWeaver.

The following two examples follow the arguments presented in (van Angeren, 2013).

Example: Open Design Alliance

Open Design Alliance is a non-profit organization of developers focusing on the development of their Teigha platform, a platform for CAD and other technical graphics applications. Today the ODA is has over 1200 members, Figure 87 provides an overview of the ODA ecosystem and describes the main interactions that take place between the Open Design Alliance, their partners and the customers of these partners.

"The main goal the ODA has with their membership model is the expansion of the Open Design Alliance software ecosystem. Another goal ODA has with their membership model is the development of their platform through co-innovation, a product related goal. The majority of membership model fees flow back into the development of Teigha and in cooperation with members new features or additional functionality can be incorporated into the platform. The ODA aims for a certain level of empowerment between members and software platform owner by creating a supportive community around the platform. In practice, this means that the Open Design Alliance strives to make members cooperate in the development of the platform or its functionality extensions." (van Angeren, 2013)

Open Design Alliance

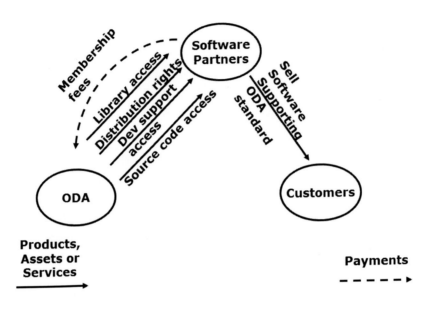

Figure 87: Standard activities in Open Design Alliance

Example: Eclipse

The Eclipse Foundation non-profit corporation providing a platform, tools and services for the Eclipse software ecosystem (van Angeren, 2013). There also is an open source community that provides frameworks and tools to support the development and deployment of software. The main goals of the Eclipse Foundation are expanding the Eclipse software ecosystem and the development of the Eclipse Foundation platform and tools.

The main interactions that take place within the Eclipse software ecosystem show up in Figure 88.

Eclipse

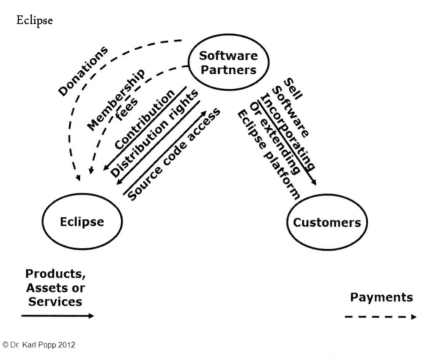

© Dr. Karl Popp 2012

Figure 88: Standard activities in Eclipse

In due diligence, there are several aspects of standards to be analysed. The use of standards, licenses for standards, contribution to standards of the target are reviewed. For post merger integration, the acquiring company must decide if they would like to continue, extend or stop the engagement of the target in standards activities.

7.10 Takeaways from chapter 7

After natural and economic ecosystems we introduced software ecosystems. You have also learned about characteristics like types of ccosystems, roles of companies in ecosystems. Modern management of and enablement of network effects is often done via online solution marketplaces, which we covered here. Many vendors also participate in stand-

Foundations of software ecosystems and their relevance for due diligence

ardization efforts to standardize markets and maximize the addressable market for their products and solutions.

In due diligence you have to create a complete and consistent view of the ecosystem activities and review the current state looking at partners, contracts, potential IP drain etc. After the review, we decide for each ecosystem activity if it should be continued, changed or discontinued. We also decide about and plan for merging ecosystems of acquirer and target.

Foundations of software ecosystems and their relevance for due diligence

8. Partnership models in the software industry

As in other industries, cooperating with partners is a key ingredient of the software business. It might even be more important than in other industries when talking about a share of fifty to ninety percent of revenue that is generated via partner channels. So in due diligence we analyze and decide about the continuation and changes to partnerships models used by the to be acquired company.

Having read this chapter, you will have an overview of partnership models and prerequisites and critical success factors of each partnership model. For each of the models, there is information about effort to be invested to create the partnership. At the end of each section in this chapter one-page cheat sheets give you hints for each of the different partnership models.

8.1   Partner categories

This chapter summarizes the types of partnerships which are typical in the software industry.

Partner categories

Usually companies in the ecosystem are summarized in the categories

❏   **Software Vendors**,

❏   **Services Partners**, including, but not limited to system integrators (SIs) partners,

❏   **Technology Partners**, which are technology vendors to provide the infrastructure for software solutions, examples are hardware vendors, database and storage vendors,

❏   **Channel Partners**, who are Value-added Resellers of specific solutions to specific markets,

- [ ] **Hosting Partners:** these are companies who are providing outsourcing and application providing services to the software vendor.

- [ ] **Support Partners:** these are partners who execute support services for the software vendor.

- [ ] **Content Partners:** these are partners who provide content, like address databases, to the software vendor.

- [ ] **Education Partners**: are partners who provide education for the software vendor´s products.

Partnership models for software vendors

Software Vendors are the focus of this book, so the emphasis will be on partnership models for Software vendors.

As a starter, let´s look at the hierarchy of partnership models that you can find in the market. There are different partnering models in the hierarchy: openly accessible partnership models and those with limited access. The first two levels of the hierarchy are limited access, but you can try to enter these levels using the advice given later in this book.

On top of the hierarchy are the partner solutions resold. It takes some effort and time to establish a reseller relationship with another software vendor. The good news: If you can make it to the status of being resold and the partner´s field organization has committed revenue numbers, it will have the chance to create a lot of revenue and to increase the valuation of your company, too.

8.2 Overview of partnership models

To get an overview without getting into too much detail, the following attributes are used to differentiate the partnerships:

- [ ] **Who ships:** The question of who ships the product is a key attribute to a partnership; shipment is often connected to a number of questions around warranty, liability and revenue recognition. It also impacts who has customer contact and control.

❑ **Pricing**: The party that sets the pricing has a huge impact on the commercial success of a partnership. Pricing also includes the handling of discounts, which leads to the resulting revenue numbers.

❑ **Branding**: Which brand will be used on the product? Which brand will be visible for customers? Who has to take the brand risk?

❑ **Intellectual Property**: Key ingredients to a partnership are the rules how to handle IP. Is joint IP intended to be created? Is there a separation of IP between the parties?

❑ **Revenue booking**: As in pricing, the revenue booking party is in control of the primary revenue stream coming from the customer.

❑ **Customer Control**: This sheds some light on the questions: What happens to the customer after the sale? Who controls the customer? Who has access to the customer to up sell products?

❑ **Go-To-Market** (GTM): This is all about who does what in marketing, pipeline management etc. Key questions are: Is the GTM done jointly or by one of the involved parties? Who carries the cost of GTM?

❑ **QA by partner**: In some cases, your partner does Quality Assurance of products to ensure high quality of products and to be able to recognize revenue.

❑ **Exclusivity**: this attribute tells if a partner has exclusive rights regarding products, customers, regions or markets.

❑ **Support** by: This gives some insight into the support channel, support cost and support obligations.

Of course there are a lot of variations of these partnership models. For the sake of simplification, we have chosen to display popular choices for attributes of the different partnerships. Each of the partnership types will be explained in one of the following chapters. The following table shows the most important attributes of the different partnership models:

	Resell	Resell Agent model	Rev Share to PARTNER	Referral Program
Who ships?	PARTNER	Software vendor	Software vendor	PARTNER
Pricing	PARTNER	PARTNER	Software vendor	PARTNER
Branding	Co- or PARTNER branded	No co-branding	No co-branding	PARTNER
IP	Separation of IP, no joint IP	Separation of IP, no joint IP	Separation of IP, no joint IP	PARTNER
Rev booking	Sold on PARTNER paper	Sold on PARTNER paper	Sold on software vendor paper	Sold on PARTNER paper
Cust. Control	PARTNER	PARTNER and software vendor	Jointly	PARTNER
GTM	PARTNER	PARTNER	Jointly	PARTNER
Exclusivity	Yes and no	Usually no	Usually no	Usually no
QA by PARTNER	Yes	No	Yes	Yes
Support by	PARTNER	Software vendor	Software vendor	Software vendor

Table 1: Partnership types Resell, revenue share and referral

Partnership models in the software industry

	OEM	Outbound OEM	Certified Solution	Dev Cooperation
Who ships?	Software vendor	PARTNER	Software vendor	Software vendor
Pricing	Software vendor	PARTNER	Software vendor	Software vendor
Branding	No co-branding	No co-branding	No co-branding	No co-branding
IP	PARTNER owns platform, software vendor own application	Software vendor owns platform, PARTNER owns application	Separation of IP, no joint IP	Separation of IP, no joint IP
Rev booking	Sold on software vendor paper	Sold on PARTNER paper	Sold on software vendor paper	Sold on software vendor paper
Cust. Control	Software vendor	PARTNER	Software vendor	Software vendor
GTM	Software vendor	PARTNER	Software vendor	Software vendor
Exclusivity	Usually no	Usually no	No	Usually no
QA by PARTNER	Yes	Yes	No	No
Support by	Software vendor support	PARTNER	Software vendor	Software vendor

Table 2: Partnership types OEM, Outbound OEM, certified solution and development cooperation

In due diligence, all contracts for all partnership types are collected and reviewed for compliance and risks. For merger integration, the acquirer has to decide if and which partnerships he would like to continue, change or discontinue. Change and discontinuation might create significant efforts in merger integration.

Partnership models in the software industry

8.3 Software vendor resells your software

Three main drivers exist for a partner to **resell** solutions: significant revenue for the partner company, solution fit and non-competitive offering; with revenue being the main driver. It is key to get revenue projections from the partner's sales organization, and then address other issues. What you need to avoid is channel conflict and any competitive issues. Competitive issues arise, when products in the portfolio of the software vendor overlap with partner products or if one of the involved sales forces behaves competitively. For a quick summary, please have a look at the cheat sheet at the end of this chapter.

Definition of Resell

Resell is a relationship between your company and a resell partner and it means the following:

- ☐ Shipment of products: the partner delivers the products to customers (full resell), you deliver the software (agent resell)

- ☐ Pricing: the partner puts product on their pricelist and determines pricing

- ☐ Branding: co-branded or partner-branded possible

- ☐ Intellectual Property (IP): partner keeps their IP, you keep your IP.

- ☐ Booking revenue: Selling on partner paper, but partner needs your help to educate sales and presales people

- ☐ Customer ownership and account control:

    - ☐ full resell: full ownership and customer control by partner, access to customers e.g. only in case of support incidents

    - ☐ agent resell: customer control by partner, shipment and support by your company.

- ☐ Go-to-market: partner goes to market with the products and you support the partner in this effort

- ❏ Exclusivity: the resell might give the right to a partner to resell exclusively in a certain geographic area or a specific market

- ❏ Marketing support: the partner does marketing for your solution on the partner´s pricelist.

- ❏ Quality Assurance: if US GAAP applies, then your software has to be tested by the partner for revenue recognition reasons.

- ❏ Support:

  - ❏ Full resell: First and second level support is usually done by the partner´s support organization, third level support by you.

  - ❏ Agent resell: all support done by you.

Figure 89 shows a full resell. The software vendor supplies the software to the resell partner. The resell partner resells the software to customers. These customers pay e. g. a license and maintenance fee for the resold software. The resell partner pays a license and maintenance fee to the software vendor.

Geographic coverage of a resell can be local (for a specific country), regional (e.g. Americas) or global. If a resell is exclusive, then the resell partner has the exclusive right to sell your products in a certain market. In case of an exclusive resell you have to have a potent resell partner, who can and will sell your products in that certain market. You have to ensure by clauses in the reseller contract that the partner will really execute on the resell, because there is no alternative for a resell partner in that market.

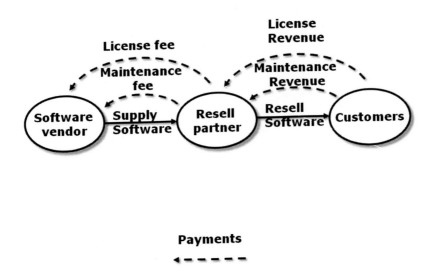

Figure 89: Resell

Requirements for Resell

The following key requirements qualify a partner solution to become a resell: the solution has a significant revenue potential for the resell partner, high minimum price tag, simplicity in packaging and licensing, financial stability, solution fit, non-competitive solution and behavior.

Significant Revenue for the partner

Revenue from reselling your products must be as high as possible. Partners are not looking at total revenue, but at the share of revenue that remains with them after deduction of the license revenue that goes to you. If the partner keeps, say, 60 percent of the resell revenue, these 60 percent have to be a lot of money. See also next section for pricing.

The Revenue Plan should to be approved (and executed later) by the partner's field organization. And there might be requirements regarding minimum company size, minimum total company revenue and other thresholds, so make sure you ask for these thresholds before you start major efforts to discuss a resell with the partner.

Example

Examples are SAP's resell of Adobe Systems products or the resell of HP's Loadrunner products by SAP. Another example is the resell of Tidal Software's datacenter automation solution for enterprise scheduling, by International Integrated Solutions, Ltd. (IIS), a leading provider of mission critical and highly available infrastructure hardware and software solutions. In the meantime, Tidal Software has been acquired by CISCO.

Minimum price tag

Ask the partner if there is a requirement for a minimum price tag. Depending on the other products sold by the partner, there might be needs to have a certain minimum price tag to get the partner's sales people the right incentive to start selling.

Make sure you get acquainted with the discount policies of the partner. Think about establishing a minimum price used for calculating the share of revenue that remains with you for a sold product. This will protect your revenue plans if there is heavy discounting done by the partner.

Simplicity in packaging and pricing

Make selling your solution by the partner as simple as possible. Start with providing small, medium and large packages and price tags. This allows a steep learning curve and easy handling of pricing for the partner's sales organization.

Financial stability

Resell partnerships usually run for at least two to three years, so financial stability of your company is key. Make sure you can prove the stability to your partner.

Solution fit

Your solution covers a whitespace in the partner's solutions that is important for the resell partner to cover. Your counterparts in the partner's business development function will ask for this, so be prepared to show that your solution is a great complement to the partner's solution portfolio.

Non-competitive solution and behavior

It is obvious that your solution resold by the partner should be non-competitive. But the rest of your product portfolio and roadmap will also be scanned carefully for competitive offerings. If there is a competitive offering, the partner's sales force will be very careful in reselling your solution and that is not good for the overall revenue.

The behavior of your sales force is a critical success factor for a successful cooperation with the partner. Make it very clear to your sales force that they should avoid competitive behavior with the partner's sales organization.

Variations of reseller relationships

Typical variations of reseller relationships are defined by recurrence and by distribution of tasks. Recurrence means if the resell takes place once or repetitively. Distribution of tasks relates to the question who is responsible for which activities in the execution of the relationship. There are many variations of resell relationships depending on the distribution of tasks between the software vendor and the resell partner. Two often used variants are full resell and agent resell.

Resell by software vendor example: Full resell

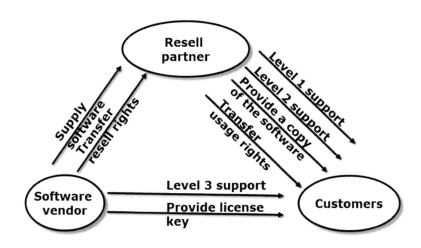

© Dr. Karl Popp 2013

Figure 90: Example for full resell relationship

Full resell

Remember what was outlined earlier in this book. Supplying software consists of providing a copy of the software, transferring usage rights and providing a license key. Support consists of providing different levels of support services to the customer. Figure 90 shows an example for the distribution of tasks in a full resell relationship.

The following table shows typical distributions of tasks in a full resell relationship:

	Tasks reside with the	
	Resell partner	Software vendor
Transfer usage rights	Always	never
Provide license key	Often	Less often
Provide level 1,2 support	Often	Less often
Provide level 3 support	Less often	Often
Shipment of releases, versions, bug fixes	Often	Less often

Figure 91: Task distribution in full resell relationships

Agent resell

In an agent resell relationship, the resell partner acts as an agent. His only task is selling the software. All other tasks remain with the software vendor. So the software vendor provides the software and support and maintenance services to the customer.

Resell by software vendor: Agent resell example

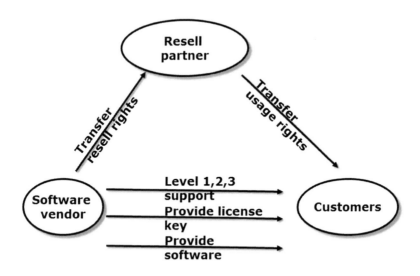

Figure 92: Task distribution in full resell relationships

As with other partnerships, the acquirer has to decide about continuing, changing or discontinuing resell partnerships. One dimension changes the analysis: the indirect relationship to the customers, especially in non-agent resell situations. This indirect relationship creates additional effort and longer timeframes for implementing changes or discontinuations of resell relationships in the post merger integration phase.

To avoid the risk of being locked out from a market, an emphasis is put on looking for exclusivity clauses in resell contracts.

8.4 System integrator resells your software

Two main drivers exist for a system integrator to resell your solutions: significant revenue from license and from services for the system integrators and solution fit with other solutions and services offered by the system integrator. It is key to get revenue projections from the partner's sales organization, and then address other issues. For a quick summary, please have a look at the cheat sheet at the end of this chapter.

Definition of Resell by System integrator

Resell is a relationship between your company and a system integrator which means the following

- ❏ Shipment of products: the system integrator delivers the products to customers

- ❏ Pricing: the system integrator puts the software vendor's product on their pricelist and determines pricing

- ❏ Branding: usually no change on branding

- ❏ Intellectual Property (IP): system integrator keeps their IP, you keep your IP.

- ❏ Booking revenue: Selling on system integrator paper, but partner needs your help to educate consultants and sales people

- ❏ Customer ownership and account control: joint ownership and customer control, access to customers in case of presales, sales activities and support incidents

- ❏ Go-to-market: system integrator goes to market with the products and you support the partner in this effort

- ❏ Exclusivity: the resell might give the right to the system integrator to resell exclusively in a certain geographic area or a specific market. This is usually not done due to focus of system integrators on service revenue, not license revenue.

- ❏ Marketing support: the system integrator does marketing for your solution on the partner's pricelist.

- ❏ Quality Assurance: if US GAAP applies, then your software has to be tested by the system integrator for revenue recognition reasons.

❐ Support: First and second level support is usually done by the system integrator, third level support by the software vendor.

The system integrator resells the software and its services to customers. These customers pay a license and maintenance fee for the resold software as well as fees for the services to the system integrator. The system integrator pays a license and maintenance fee to the software vendor.

The following figure shows the software vendor supplying the software to the system integrator.

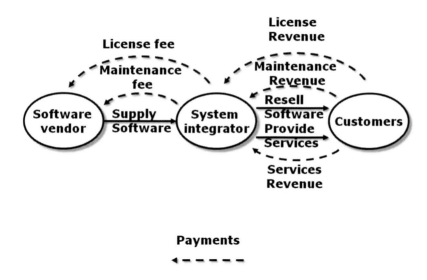

Figure 93: Resell by system integrator

Since the system integrator sells services and software, prices for both compete for the customer revenue, so the software price tag might be under pressure. So make sure you know about how much service revenue is generated per each license revenue dollar to negotiate a good deal.

Partnership models in the software industry

Geographic coverage of a Resell can be local (for a specific country), regional (Americas) or global. If a resell is exclusive, then the resell partner has the exclusive right to sell your products in a certain market. An exclusive resell should not be pursued. This would impose a high risk on the software vendor, since the focus of the system integrator is on service revenue and not on license revenue. In addition, the license revenue scales with the number of related projects of the system integrator. To massively increase sales of the software, the number of related projects must grow dramatically or the number of consultants of the system integrator must grow dramatically. Both are usually not the case.

Requirements for Resell by system integrator

The following key requirements qualify a partner solution to become a resell: the solution has a significant license and service revenue potential for the resell partner and there is solution fit with the other solutions and services offered by the system integrator.

Significant Revenue for the partner

Revenue from services around your solution and from licenses reselling your products must be as high as possible. So evaluation of the opportunity is done based on combined revenue. System integrators are looking at total combined license and services revenue. This total revenue might include license and services from other solutions, too, if the system integrator sells and end-to-end solution including services to a customer.

The Revenue Plan should to be approved (and executed later) by the system integrator's sales organization. And there might be minimum company size, minimum total company revenue and other thresholds, so make sure you ask for these thresholds before you start major efforts to discuss a resell with the system integrator.

Example

An example for a system integrator reselling software is Teleca Limited, a leading pan-European Systems Integrator. They resell IT Au-

tomation software from Opsware Inc.. Another example is Microsoft's reseller program for Microsoft Dynamics targeted at system integrators.

Solution fit

Your solution fits one of the areas of expertise of the system integrator's services offering. The system integrator is focused on services revenue. So make sure you can show how much service revenue is generated per license revenue dollar.

Your counterparts in business development will ask for this, so be prepared to show that your solution is a great complement to the partner's solution portfolio and that there is significant services revenue attached with it.

> In due diligence, all resell contracts are reviewed both from a legal point of view, but also from an ecosystem strategy point of view. To avoid the risk of being locked out from a market, an emphasis is put on looking for exclusivity clauses in resell contracts.

8.5 Revenue share from a software vendor to the partner

The hierarchy of partnerships contains partner solutions that are sold by the software vendor, but a revenue share goes to the partner to compensate for joint go-to-market. There might be global, regional and local revenue shares. This chapter gives the software vendor all the details.

Definition of Revenue share

Revenue share from the software vendor to the partner is defined as follows:

❏ Shipment of products: the software vendor ships the product to the customers

- ❏ Pricing: The software vendor have the product on its pricelist and you determine the pricing

- ❏ Branding: the software vendor's branding stays as defined, no co-branding possible

- ❏ IP: the software vendor keeps its IP, the partners keep their IP

- ❏ Booking revenue: Selling on the software vendor's paper, but the software vendor has to give a share of revenue to the partner

- ❏ Customer ownership and account control: joint ownership and customer control by the partner and the software vendor

- ❏ Go-to-market: joint go-to-market taking most of the work, sharing of pipelines on both sides is possible

- ❏ Marketing: the revenue share partner does some marketing.

- ❏ Quality Assurance: For revenue recognition reasons the software vendor's software might have to be tested by the revenue share partner.

- ❏ Support: First, second and third level support is done by the software vendor. There is a joint support agreement in place that organizes the cooperation with the revenue share partner's support in case there has to be a joint work on customer support incidents.

In a revenue share situation, the revenue share partner endorses the software vendor's solution at the customers. If the software vendor sells to revenue share partner's customers, the software vendor pays a revenue share to the revenue share partner.

One important point here is margin considerations. Since the revenue share partner gets a share of the software vendor's revenue while cost of product being almost constant, your margin for the product might decrease dramatically, if the revenue is not high enough. The software vendor has to make sure to calculate a best case and a worst case scenario of the business case including margin considerations.

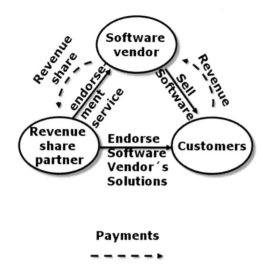

Revenue Share

Figure 94: Revenue share

Example

Examples of revenue shares are SAP's Endorsed Business Solutions. SAP gets revenue shares from Streamserve for Financial Solutions or from Meridium with RCMO™ (Reliability Centered Maintenance and Optimization).

Requirements for revenue share

The following requirements apply for revenue share :

Appropriate Sales organization

Since the software vendor has to sell the solution they should have an appropriate sales organization in place or you should be able to show

Partnership models in the software industry

how they would like to grow their organization with revenue growth. The revenue share partner will look very carefully if the sales numbers correspond with the number of sales people in the software vendor's organization.

Significant Revenue for revenue share partner and for the software vendor

The revenue share for the revenue share partner must be as high as possible. Revenue share partners are not looking at total revenue, but at the share of revenue that remains with them after deduction the license revenue that goes to the software vendor. If the revenue share partner keeps, say, 40 percent of product revenue, these 40 percent have to be a lot of money. See also next section for pricing.

Although the software vendor is selling, the Revenue Plan has to be approved by the revenue share partner's field organization. And the revenue share partner might have defined minimum company size, minimum total company revenue and other thresholds, so make sure to ask for these thresholds before you start major efforts to discuss a revenue share with the revenue share partner. Make sure you have an eye on your margin as stated above.

Minimum price tag

The entry price tag should be suiting the needs of the revenue share partner's sales organization and prize ranges of the revenue share partner's product portfolio. Some sales teams are used to high price tags and thus motivation of that sales team requires high entry price tags. The software vendor should also analyze discounting practices. A high price tag is also needed to compensate for any discounts.

Simplicity in packaging and pricing

Make positioning your solution by the partner as simple as possible. Start with providing small, medium and large packages and price tags. This allows a steep learning curve and easy handling of pricing for sales.

Financial stability

Revenue share partners want long-term relationships with partners and customers, so financial stability is key. Partnerships usually run for at least three years.

> For due diligence, revenue share agreements carry limited risk due to the direct relationship of the software vendor with the customer. To avoid the risk of being locked out from a market, an emphasis is put on looking for exclusivity clauses in revenue share contracts.

8.6   Referral programs

If a partner provides a lead to the software vendor and the software vendor closes a deal with this customer, a referral fee is paid to the partner by the software vendor. A Referral program has a very low entry barrier and low maintenance effort. This chapter provides you with all the details.

Definition of a Referral program

A referral program is defined as follows:

- ❏ Shipment of products: software vendor ships the product to the customers;
- ❏ Pricing: software vendor determines the pricing;
- ❏ Branding: products remains branded as is;
- ❏ IP: software vendor keeps his IP, partner keeps his IP;
- ❏ Booking revenue: Selling on software vendor paper, but partner gets a referral fee from software vendor;

Partnership models in the software industry

- ☐ Customer ownership and account control: shared ownership and customer control by the partner and the software vendor;

- ☐ Go-to-market: sharing of customer opportunities from partner, to software vendor;

- ☐ Marketing: no defined marketing;

- ☐ Quality Assurance: software vendor does QA for his products;

- ☐ Support: No support obligations for referral partner.

Referral Program

Figure 95: Referral Program

As stated in an earlier chapter, Referral means that a software vendor outsources lead generation to a partner for a referral fee. A Referral Program rewards the referral of leads from a partner to the software vendor. Depending on the sales organization of the software vendor, the program

Partnership models in the software industry

might be available for specific products and in specific countries. After enrolling to the program, a partner under the Referral program forwards a lead to the software vendor.

The next step is with the software vendor to accept the lead. If the lead is accepted, then the software vendor will provide the referral fee to the partner. The payment of referral fees can be step by step. In some agreements the payment arrangements say that a first referral fee is paid to the partner on providing the lead. If the lead results in a license purchase, then the software vendor will pay a percentage of the license revenue to the partner as a second referral fee.

Example

One example of a referral program is the SAP Referral Program. Deals are numerous and can be found on SAP's web pages about the referral program.

Requirements for a Referral Program

The following requirements apply for a Referral program:

Availability of program by country or region

Availability of the program has to be defined by country and region as well as by products that are applicable for the Referral program.

8.7   Online partner solution marketplace

Large software vendors usually offer an online partner solution marketplace. Customers of the large software vendor gather there to look for complementing solutions from partners. Partners have the opportunity to advertise partner solutions exactly where customers are looking for the solutions of the large software vendor.

Partnership models in the software industry

Definition of online partner solution marketplace

Online partner solution marketplaces are marketplaces on the internet operated by a large software vendor to advertise partner solutions. Besides the solution name, partners can include collaterals, success stories and whitepapers on this site.

Customers can look up and select partner solutions on the website of the marketplace. Online reviews and ratings of the solutions and links to additional information about the solutions complete the information provided on such a marketplace.

Once a customer is interested in a solution, the customer enters his contact data and the software vendor forwards this contact data to the partner.

Online partner solution marketplace participation means the following:

☐ Shipment of products: Partner ships products.

☐ Pricing: Partner determines pricing.

☐ Branding: partner-branded only.

☐ Intellectual Property (IP): Software vendor keeps its IP; you keep your IP as a partner.

☐ Booking revenue: Selling on partner paper.

☐ Customer ownership and account control: full ownership and customer control by you. The software vendor forwards the customer request for buying to you.

☐ Go-to-market: The software vendor offers the opportunity to advertise, no additional go-to-market attached.

☐ Marketing support: No marketing support except advertising space.

☐ Quality Assurance: You test your software.

☐ Support: Support is done by you for your solutions.

Examples for online partner solution catalogues are Microsoft´s Partner Solution Finder or the Ecosystem Hub by SAP or Apple´s Appstore.

Partnership models in the software industry

Example

Ecosystem Hub is a global partnership model from SAP, which contains an online partner solution marketplace. Partners can get advertising space on SAP's global website http://ecohub.sap.com. Customers are able to browse SAP's solution offering and can find your advertised solution, too. Customers and partners can also attach ratings and reviews to the advertised products. If customers want to buy a product, SAP collects the lead information and forwards it to the partner.

SAP's goal for this partnership model is maximizing the revenue from platform user licenses and maximizing the platform adoption of SAP's NetWeaver platform. Platform User Licenses are licenses sold by SAP to customers when customers run partner solutions on the SAP NetWeaver platform. Requirements are SAP partner edge membership, SAP certified solution, Platform User License Certification, EcoHub Participation Agreement signed.

Recently, SAP enabled system integrators to show their offerings on SAP Ecohub, too.

Figure 96 shows the services and payments flowing for an online solution marketplace. Customers pay a license and maintenance fee for the software sold by the partner. The partner may pay fees for advertising on the online partner solution marketplace.

Partnership models in the software industry

Online partner solution marketplace

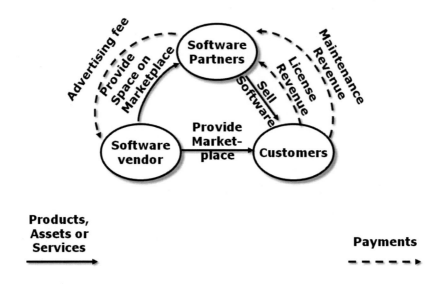

Figure 96: Online partner solution marketplace

Example

Microsoft has a website called Partner Solution Finder, where cus-
tomers can find partner solutions and services. Customers can reach
out directly to the partner, if they are interested in buying a partner
solution.

Requirements for online partner solution marketplace

The following key requirements usually apply to be listed on an online
partner solution marketplace:

☐   Membership in a partner program of the software vendor,

☐   Partner has an integrated/certified solution,

Partnership models in the software industry

❏ An agreement for listing on online partner solution marketplace is signed.

For you as a partner, the solution has to have a significant revenue potential in the customer space. The software vendor will also watch if you have a non-competitive solution and you show non-competitive behavior.

Solution fit

Your solution covers a whitespace that is important for customers. Be prepared to show that your solution is a great complement to the large software vendor´s solutions.

Non-competitive solution and behavior

It is obvious that your solution on the online solution marketplace of the software vendor should be non-competitive. But the rest of your product portfolio and roadmap will also be scanned carefully for competitive offerings. If there is a competitive offering, the software vendor will be very careful in advertising your solution and that is not good for overall revenue.

Example

Apple´s Appstore does not allow apps that are selling other apps to ensure non-competitive offerings.

The behavior of your sales force is also key for a successful cooperation with the software vendor. Make it very clear to your sales force that they should avoid competitive behavior with sales people of the software vendor.

In due diligence the business model, the revenue and profitability as well as the contractual situation of a target´s online partner solution marketplace are diligently analyzed. The acquirer has to decide if the marketplace should be changed, continued, discontinued and plan accordingly for merger integration.

8.8 Outbound OEM

You might want to increase the number of customers using your technology as part of your partner's solutions. For this purpose, software companies license software to partners (e. g. other software vendors). With the license, the partner ships their software including the software licensed from the software vendor to their customers.

Definition of Outbound OEM

Outbound OEM is defined as follows:

☐ Shipment of products: the partner ships his product to the customers including the OEM software of the software vendor.

☐ Pricing: Partner has a product on his pricelist and he determines the pricing, the OEM software is included in this product.

☐ Branding: Partner's branding can apply (white label OEM) or the branding of the OEM remains unchanged.

☐ IP: Partner keeps his IP, software vendor keeps his IP.

☐ Booking revenue: Selling on Partner paper.

☐ Customer ownership and account control: ownership and customer control by the partner.

☐ Go-to-market: go-to-market by the partner.

☐ Quality Assurance: For revenue recognition reasons your software has to be tested by the partner.

☐ Support: First and second level support is done by the partner. Third level support for the OEM software is done by the software vendor.

Partnership models in the software industry

OEM

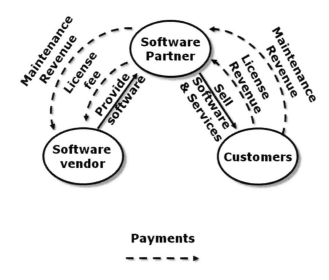

Figure 97: Outbound OEM

Outbound OEM means that a software company licenses software to a partner and the partner ships their software including the software licensed from the software vendor to their customers.

Figure 97 explains the software shipments and revenue streams. The software vendor delivers the OEM software to the partner, which pays a license fee and maintenance fee to the software vendor. The license fee might be a share of the revenue of the partner product containing the OEM software. Or it might be a constant fee that applies per copy of the OEM software shipped to the customer.

The software partner sells its applications including the OEM software to customers. The customer pays a license and maintenance fee to the partner company.

Page 237

Partnership models in the software industry

Example

An OEM example for SAP is Callataÿ & Wouters. They have an OEM relationship for SAP's banking platform. Callataÿ & Wouters plans to include SAP's banking platform into its Thaler solution.

Microsoft has numerous OEM relationships. Examples are their OEM relationships with hardware vendors. Hardware vendors like HP include the Windows operating system in their computer systems sold to customers.

Requirements for Outbound OEM

The following requirements apply for Outbound OEM:

Solution fit

Make sure there is solution fit with the partner's product portfolio and your entry price tag and/or market coverage of relevant markets is high.

Process to get an outbound OEM

There is a process to work on creating an OEM contract. If needed, get help from partner consulting companies like Synomic, who can provide guidance and assistance along the process.

Contact the partner. Make sure you identify the business owners and contact them first. Show them how your solution fits their product portfolio and how it creates value for the software vendor. Try to find out if they are interested. The partner might have minimum requirements for company size, company revenue etc. of an OEM partner. So ask for these minimum requirements and if you match these requirements.

8.9 Certified Interface partnerships

Chapter summary

Often, customers will ask for integration certification of your solution before they consider your solution for purchase. To prove, that your solu-

Partnership models in the software industry

tion is properly integrated with a software vendor's solution, software vendors usually offer a certification process and an attached partnership model. In most cases the software vendor's partner carries the cost to build the integration and the cost for certification.

Definition of Certified solutions

Certified solutions are defined as follows:

☐ Shipment of products: you ship the product to the customers.

☐ Pricing: You have the product on your pricelist and you determine the pricing.

☐ Branding: your branding stays as defined by you, no co-branding possible. Logo usage of a specific logo for certified partners might be included.

☐ IP: Software vendor keeps its IP, you keep your IP.

☐ Booking revenue: Selling on your paper, no revenue share goes to the software vendor.

☐ Customer ownership and account control: ownership and customer control by you.

☐ Go-to-market: usually no joint go-to-market, but other partnership models might apply, like online partner solution marketplace.

☐ Marketing: The software vendor might allow logo usage of a certification logo. You have the opportunity to release your own press release about certification.

☐ Quality Assurance: You do QA for your solutions.

☐ Support: First, second and third level support is done by you.

Certification usually is the entry ticket to more advanced partnerships. So it is a good starter to test the opportunities in the ecosystem of a software vendor with limited investment and limited risk. Figure 98 shows how it works. The software vendor provides certification services for a certification fee and logo usage to software companies. Software companies sell their software to customers. No revenue share is paid to the software vendor.

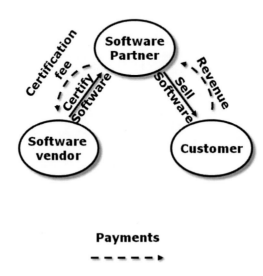

Figure 98: Certified Solution

Example

SAP has created a Certification process and organization that ensures interface testing of partner solutions. SAP has lots of interfaces to choose from. If the certification process is successful, you will receive a logo, which approves that you have run successfully through certification.

One example for a SAP certified solution is LogicTools's network design solution. LogicNet Plus can be used as an extension to the SAP

Partnership models in the software industry

Supply Chain Management solution and has a certified integration with SAP.

Requirements for Certification

The following requirement applies for certification:

Realistic usage scenario

Technical integration of your solution with the software vendor's solutions must make sense to customers. There must be a realistic usage scenario for customers using your solution together with the software vendor's solution.

In due diligence we analyze all certifications of the target company and determine the impact of the acquisition on the certifications, because certifications might not be automatically transferred to the acquirer during merger integration.

8.10 Software Development Cooperations

Chapter summary

If a software company works with a partner to e.g. define and test new interfaces, a Software Development Cooperation agreement is signed. It basically says that the software company and the partner work together to define the interface owned by the partner and that the software company will build an application against this interface and work together with the partner on testing the interface and the application build on top of it. Both companies have engineering work and cost. Usually the engineering cost is split between the companies.

Example

One example for a Software Development Cooperation is the publicly announced relationship between SAP and Amberpoint. Amberpoint works with SAP in the area of SOA management and SOA governance.

Both companies have engineering work and cost to build the integration.

Definition of Software Development Cooperations

Software Development Cooperations are defined as follows:

- ☐ Shipment of products: you ship the product to the customers.

- ☐ Pricing: You have the product on your pricelist and you determine the pricing.

- ☐ Branding: your branding stays as defined by you, no co-branding possible. Logo usage is not included.

- ☐ IP: Software vendor keeps its IP, you keep your IP.

- ☐ Booking revenue: Selling on your paper, no revenue share goes to the software vendor.

- ☐ Customer ownership and account control: ownership and customer control by you.

- ☐ Go-to-market: no joint go-to-market with you taking most of the work, no sharing of pipelines on both sides, exceptions to the rule are possible.

- ☐ Marketing: usually very little marketing for you by the software vendor.

- ☐ Quality Assurance: You do QA for your solutions.

- ☐ Support: First, second and third level support is done by you.

Partnership models in the software industry

Software Development Cooperation

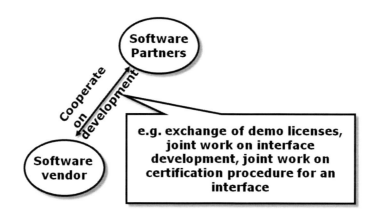

Figure 99: Software Development Cooperation

Requirements

Solution fit

Make sure there is solution fit with SAP product portfolio. Then the desired integration between your solution and the software vendor´s solution makes sense.

Dedicated skilled resources

The idea is that you integrate your solution with the software vendor´s solution and that you are able to support the integration as well. In order to be able to do that, you have to have skilled development, consulting and support resources.

Page 243

Partnership models in the software industry

8.11 Takeaways from chapter 8

In this chapter we have learned about details of partner relationships in the software industry and their impact on due diligence activities. Since partner ecosystems are important for success and since even small software vendors usually engage in numerous partner activities, the due diligence of partner relationships creates a high workload for the due diligence team. A special focus is put on risks of partner relationships with exclusivity being a major risk.

9. Summary and conclusion

With the knowledge aggregated in this book, you should now have the foundational skills to prepare for due diligence of software companies. As mentioned before, it is paramount to have the basic skills about the M&A process, types of due diligence and the specific business models of the software industry to be a successful acquirer of a software business.

These are the prerequisites and success factors for successful due diligence that you have learned in this book:

☐ **M&A process**: establish a process template and get at least on level 3 of the M&A process maturity and capability model; shape your process based on the process template in chapter 3.4. Plan and execute merger integration due diligence in addition to target due diligence.

☐ **M&A organization**: make sure you have dedicated, full time people involved and sufficient staffing to carry out due diligence and post merger integration workload. If needed, get help from external advisors and consultants.

☐ **M&A experience management:** Leverage the experiences from past acquisitions to improve all aspects of your M&A organization, process, likelihoods etc.

☐ **Due diligence coverage**: Make sure you cover all types of due diligence in a coherent model, not just a subset. Make merger integration planning and merger integration due diligence an equally important part of due diligence.

☐ **Risk detection and management**: Use the approach from chapter 5 and a list of risks to completely capture risks and manage them properly.

☐ **Due diligence hacks**: Use the eight laws of due diligence from chapter 1.5 to avoid pitfalls.

❏ Be aware of the **specifics of the software business**, its business and revenue models (chapter 6) as well as its software ecosystem specifics (chapter 7), including all possible partnership models (chapter 8).

So I hope you enjoyed this book and I am looking forward to have you look at part 2 of this book as well.

Discuss and share your feedback at http://www.mergerduediligence.com.

Follow me on twitter @karl_popp. https://twitter.com/karl_popp

Connect with me on linkedin: de.linkedin.com/in/drkarlmichaelpopp/

10. Bibliography

Beiners, D., Burmeister, F., Tries, H.-J. 2009. *Mergers and Acquisitions in Germany.* München : C.H.Beck, 2009.

Berens, W., Brauner, H.U., Strauch, J. 2008. *Due diligence bei Unternehmensakquisitionen.* Stuttgart : Schäfer Poeschel, 2008.

Bruner, R.F., Levitt, A.,. 2009. *Deals from Hell: M&A Lessons that Rise Above the Ashes.* Hoboken : Wiley, 2009.

Buxmann, P., Hess, T., Diefenbach, H. 2012. *The Software Industry.* Berlin : Springer, 2012.

CMMI_Product_Team. 2010. *CMMI® for Development, Version 1.3.* Hanscom : s.n., 2010.

Ferstl, O. K., Sinz, E. J. 1997. Modeling of Business Systems Using the Semantic Object Model (SOM) - A Methodological Framework. In: P., Schmidt, Bernus. *Handbook of architecture of information systems.* New York : Springer, 1997.

Gerds, J., Schewe, G. 2010. *Post Merger Integration: Unternehmenserfolg durch Integration Excellence.* Berlin : Springer, 2010.

Kude, T. 2012. *The Coordination of Inter-Organizational Networks in the Enterprise Software Industry: The Perspective of Complementors .* Pieterlen : Peter Lang, 2012.

Meyer, R. 2010. *Partnering with SAP.* Norderstedt : BOD, 2010.

Meyer, R., Popp, K.M. 2011. *Profit from software ecosystems.* Norderstedt : BOD, 2011.

Picot, G. 2005. *Handbuch Mergers and Acquisitions.* Stuttgart : Poeschel, 2005.

Popp, K.M. 2011. *Advances in software business.* Norderstedt : BOD, 2011.

Smith, K., Reed Layoux, A. 2012. *M&A Strategy.* New York : McGraw Hill, 2012.

van Angeren, J., Kabbedijk, J., Popp, K.M.,. 2013. Managing Software Ecosystems through Partnering. In: S., Cusumano, M., Jansen, S. Brinkkemper. *Software ecosystems.* Cheltenham : Edward Elgar, 2013.

Waltl, J. 2013. *Intellectual Property Modularity in Software Products and Software Platform Ecosystems.* Norderstedt : Books on demand, 2013.

Weill, P., Malone, T. W., D'Urso, V. T., Herman, G., Woerner, S. 2005. *Do Some Business Models Perform Better than Others? A Study of the 1000 Largest US Firms.* Boston : MIT Center for Coordination Science, 2005. Working Paper No. 226.

Bibliography

11. Advertising

DRKARLPOPP.COM M&A videos

Based on this book, i have created videos on due diligence, post merger integration, risk management, IP management and many other topics. many more. The objective is to provide software business education for software executives online at
http://www.drkarlpopp.com/softwareecosystemvideos.html .

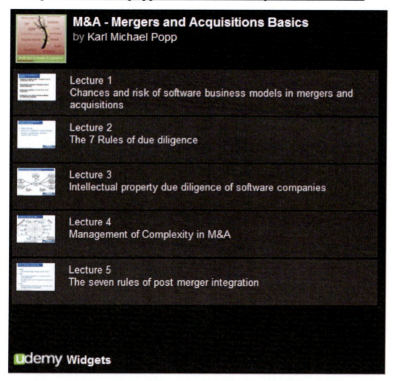

Education using videos is cheap, convenient and effective. Please use the link below to access the videos. Try them today! You can find my M&A education videos on
http://www.udemy.com/ma-mergers-and-acquisitions-basics/.

Page 249

Book: Partnering with SAP

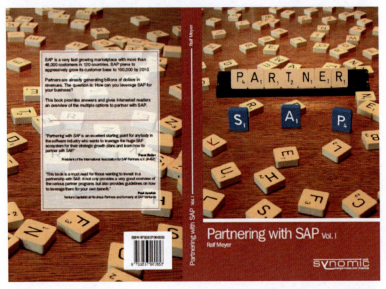
Advertising

Book: Profit from Software Ecosystems

Advertising

Book: Advances in software business

Karl Michael Popp (ed.)

Advances in software business

This book is targeted at people interested in leading edge research on software ecosystems like partner managers, business developers, but also students and researchers in information systems and software business.

This book contains key **research articles** on the subject of the software business. Taken from conferences like the International conference on the software business and journals like IEEE Software, you get the latest and greatest information on the topic.

The book is available on Amazon (ISBN: 978-3-8448-0405-8), on iTunes and for Kindle.

For more information: www.advancesinsoftwarebusiness.com

SOFTWARE-IP.COM website

Page 253

DRKARLPOPP.COM website

Advertising

DRKARLPOPP.COM Software business videos

Advertising

Synomic

Synomic www.synomic.com is a boutique management consultancy and was founded in 2006 by Software and SAP Ecosystem experts. Focus is on Alliance Management, Business Development and Corporate Development consulting including Go-to-Market (GTM) and the support of the Venture Capital funding process.

Tailored offerings address the specific needs of Software Companies:

- ☐ Leverage the huge SAP Ecosystem for GTM and business success
- ☐ Implement or improve a winning SAP Partnering Strategy
- ☐ Go-to-Market in Germany/Europe/USA with or without focus on the SAP Ecosystem
- ☐ Corporate development including the support for the Venture (VC) Funding process
- ☐ SAP and IT partnering know-how and best practices
- ☐ Support for marketing and sales (channel/direct)
- ☐ Coaching for teaming with SAP and other IT ecosystems

Benefits include

- ☐ More productive partnering & business relationships
- ☐ Increased focus on core competencies
- ☐ Quicker scaling of business with reduced overall costs and risk

Examples of Services

- ☐ Service SAP Ecosystem Strategy
    - ☐ Assessment and strategy development
    - ☐ Business and partnering models
    - ☐ Market and white space analysis
- ☐ Corporate Development
    - ☐ Support of the venture capital (VC) funding process

- ☐ Go-to-market strategy development
- ☐ Interim Corporate Development
☐ Business Development
- ☐ Market and white space analysis including feasibility studies
- ☐ Support the implementation and execution of business plans
- ☐ Go-to-market in Germany including sales support
- ☐ Interims Business Development
☐ Synomic "Partner Incubator"
- ☐ Virtual presence @ SAP in Walldorf
- ☐ Orchestration of services provided by Synomic partners
- ☐ Business Start in Germany

Contact:

Synomic GmbH
Altrottstrasse 31
SAP Partner-Port
69190 Walldorf
info@synomic.com
Phone: +49-(0)6227-73-2455
Fax: +49-(0)6227-73-2459

12.   Index

Index